Vegan

JUNK FOOD

A down and dirty cookbook

Zacchary Bird

Vegan
JUNK FOOD
A down and dirty cookbook

Smith
Street
Books

Dear Readers,

As veganism has surged in popularity over the past few years, so have the variety of people interested in vegan food. I've cooked for them all: retreats full of people with different dietary requirements finally able to share the same meals, large crowds of vegans wanting to try quirky deep-fried dishes, classes of all ages trying to pick up new kitchen skills, small families trying to make the switch, lines of hungry festival goers who couldn't care less what they're served as long as it's delicious, plus friends and family. All were guinea pigs for the recipes in this book – the dishes you'll learn to make within these pages are confirmed hits across all demographics.

This is a vegan cookbook and veganism is not a diet: you can be a junk food vegan, environmentalist vegan, ethical vegan, a quiet vegan, a loud vegan or even a healthy vegan (although that last kind won't find much solace and I think we've got enough bliss ball recipes by now). These recipes aim to show you how to mimic the most indulgent dishes from around the world without using any animals. With this book in hand, you can transform your kitchen into your favourite fast-food joints or liven up the smorgasbord at parties (pending being invited to any). Those who think they hate vegan food just haven't yet figured out how to cook vegetables properly, so if this is you it's time to learn. It's lucky you've picked up the right book. Whether you want a substitute for your favourite greasy burger, or you've got a point to prove and want to make an entire chicken drumstick including a bone from scratch, you'll find it here.

So, why would a vegan go to so much effort to recreate the precise dishes they aim to avoid? Food is cultural, and we crave our favourite familiar meals. The eating of animals, however, is not a culture that can be appropriated. Animal-based dishes do not have a monopoly on flavours, textures or shapes. It's all open season. Anything can be made vegan, and it should! I've heard every reason for choosing a plant-based diet and it's very rare that someone made the switch because they didn't enjoy the flavours of animal products – so if we can recreate them, why not? When Blumenthal turns meat into a fruit, the world can't applaud loudly enough. Visionary! When vegans do the opposite, apparently we've got a lot of bloody nerve. Creative cooks around the world have made it so that you don't need to miss out on the flavours you love by choosing the vegan option, and that's something to celebrate.

Plant-based food has no limits, and with the advent of so many new products there's no need to be alarmed by references to animal products in this book. Ingredients, such as beef- and chicken-style stock, vegan fish sauce, dairy-free butter, cheese and so on have all become incredibly easy to find. The ingredients guide on the following pages will explain the rest.

Ingredients guide

Agar agar

Algae-derived and the perfect substitute for gelatine, agar agar comes in powdered or flake form, the former being what the recipes in this book use.

Alcohol

There are resources aplenty on the internet to check if your alcohol is vegan. The main one to watch out for is wine, which is often fined using egg, milk or isinglass. Guinness stout is called for to make the Bratwurst on page 82, as their recipe has changed to a vegan version in recent years.

Aquafaba

Remarkably versatile, the brine in a tin of beans is a miracle egg replacer. The liquid works from tinned or soaked dried chickpeas (garbanzo beans), butter beans, kidney beans and black beans (only use for dark-coloured recipes like chocolate brownies), tofu and more. It can mimic an egg in almost any application, including egging someone you don't like (particularly effective if you leave the liquid in the tin!). This versatility extends to Scrabble™ where it is now an official word and the perfect excuse to use up your Qs, Fs and Bs. As a loose rule, three tablespoons of aquafaba will replace one egg in baked recipes.

Banana blossom

Your best bet at finding this will be the tinned version in an Asian supermarket.

It's weird, kind of gross and doesn't look very appealing. So it's perfect for mimicking seafood. Only use fresh banana blossom if you're looking for a summer project and not if you intend to have a quick, easy meal.

Cheese

At home, things that will help you recreate 'cheesy' flavours include nutritional yeast, white miso paste, Dijon mustard, rejuvelac or just being vegan long enough that you forget what real cheese tastes like.

Store-bought vegan feta varies in ingredients and quality. The lower end ones are oil-based and can, brand-to-brand, sometimes work nicely but they are inconsistent. Tofu or nut-based cultivated cheeses, albeit usually more expensive, perform much better when making veganised versions of feta-based dishes.

Chickpea flour

A serial offender of being served undercooked, resulting in bitter and unpalatable food. When prepared properly, this magic ingredient does the heavy lifting in Seitan chickpea chicken (see page 163) and Spanakopita (see page 102), and helps to bind the Falafel on page 162. It's sometimes called gram flour and besan, but check the ingredients if yours is sold under the besan name as it might be cut with a little split-pea flour. If so, you'll need to use extra for your recipe (approx. 1:1.25 if using a brand with split-pea flour). Try mixing chickpea flour and water (1:1) and frying for quick flatbread.

Fish sauce

Vegan versions can be found at specialty stores and, more recently, some Asian supermarkets. If you can't source it, replace with soy sauce or just leave out.

Flaxseeds (linseeds)

The O.G. egg replacer. Mixed with water, the resulting gel works in most recipes that call for an egg for binding purposes. Bonus round: flaxseeds are a rare vegan source of omega-3.

Gluten flour/Vital wheat gluten

One of the best sources of vegan protein, but it gets little credit. It's essentially flour with everything but the gluten washed away. The chewy strands that come from kneading are the foundation for many fake meats.

Gums (Guar/Xanthan)

Thickening agents. In short, guar is better for cold dishes and xanthan for dishes that will be heated. Blend in to your recipes, or mix well with the oil component before adding them in to make sure they're properly dispersed. Add a pinch of xanthan gum to failed sauces to help them thicken up.

Honey

The most delicious and marketable of all the animal vomits. A bee can make up to half a teaspoon of honey in its lifetime, but you can make a whole batch in one lazy afternoon with my Vegan honey recipe on page 170. Alternatively, use date or rice malt syrup.

Kala namak (Indian black salt)

Powdered fart. Used to add 'eggy' flavour and scent to vegan recipes. Scrambled tofu goes from bland to suspiciously realistic with just a pinch of this.

Lactic acid

Great for adding cheesy sourness into recipes, food-grade lactic acid can be a little tricky to source, so you may need to resort to the internet. If you can't find it, substitute with a far smaller portion of the easier-to-find citric acid.

Liquid smoke

Great for introducing smoky flavours to vegan dishes where the ingredients we choose aren't cooked long enough to pick up that flavour naturally. Liquid smoke can be found at barbecue stores. Use sparingly – only add a drop at a time.

Ingredients guide

Milk

As a general rule, if you can read this sentence you're too old to be drinking real milk. Milk alternatives include: soy, coconut, almond, hazelnut, oat, hemp, spelt and more. Soy and coconut are my top choices for replacing real milk's purpose in a recipe. Soy milk, in particular, is one of the best substitutes for real milk as the fat droplets are suspended in the liquid, lending it better to creamy dishes that rely on milk's fat distribution. Use soy milk powder (found in health-food stores) to thicken creams and ice creams without adding extra liquid. If there was any truth to the myth that drinking soy gives men breasts, I'd look a hell of a lot better in a crop top by now.

MSG

Think sugar's umami cousin, this flavour enhancer really helps replicate pre-vegan flavours. While it has been demonised as being unhealthy, most research has concluded that it is perfectly safe for human consumption so get into it. You can buy it at most Asian supermarkets, but if you can't find it, torula yeast is nutritional yeast's less-beloved sibling that works like a flavour enhancer, adds meaty undertones and is probably just as difficult to source as MSG anyway.

Mustard

Pretty much always vegan. Dijon mustard classically uses wine or verjuice in the filtering process which might not be vegan (see Alcohol note) however most readily available brands are in the clear, and a polite message to your local mustard maker is all it takes to check.

Nutritional yeast (Nooch)

The holy grail ingredient. Available in flakes or powder, this stuff tastes vaguely like a smoky cheese and is responsible for most homemade vegan cheese flavours. To boot, many brands fortify their nutritional yeast with B12, and with it being naturally full of the other B complex vitamins, 'nooch' (as it is affectionately called) is an asset to anyone's pantry. Alternative sources of B12 include an oral spray or toothpaste, occasional injection, adding a teaspoon of dirt to your morning smoothie, feeding a supplement to cattle and then eating them (the natural way), or just forgetting to take your supplement and then taking a handful every few days like the rest of us.

Stock

Many grocery stores now sell vegan beef- and chicken-style stocks; however, if you can't find them then good old vegetable or mushroom stock isn't the worst thing in the world. On that note, many soup recipes are delicious with only water instead of using the same stock as a base for all your soups.

TVP

Textured Vegetable Protein. It comes in a huge variety of shapes and textures to lend itself to many different kinds of meat. Most of the recipes in this book utilise the small chunks or mince. This is one of the most common faux meats available, and can be rehydrated in water, stock or a flavoured broth before being used as you would meat in cooking.

Worcestershire sauce

Classically made using anchovies, you can usually find an animal product–free Worcestershire sauce at most supermarkets, and it's usually the cheaper one, too.

Yoghurt

Try your local options to see what doesn't suck. Depending on where you are, this may be made from coconut, almond, soy or oat. Whichever one you choose, the thicker the better for the recipes in this book.

A note on deep-frying

This book makes good use of the only oils that are truly essential in life: the ones you use to deep-fry in. Pick an oil with a high smoke point, as you'll be frying at high temperatures. Rapeseed, sunflower, vegetable blends, peanut or canola oil are all great choices. If you've got a kitchen thermometer handy, it's as simple as making sure your oil is above 180°C (350°F) before adding your ingredients. If you don't have a thermometer, less precise methods include adding a pinch of salt (which will sizzle) or a wooden skewer (which will vigorously bubble) to the hot oil to see if it's reached the right temperature. Any thoughts to add a splash of water to the oil will result in an attempt on your life.

DIPS AND SNACKS

This chapter puts your deep-frying skills to good use by frying all manner of ingredients in sizzling oil. Start with something simple like fried pickles or fried green tomatoes, then take it up a level with jalapeno poppers and mozzarella sticks. The final challenge is tackling the deep-fried lasagne, which is just as delicious as how you're imagining it to be.

Of course, not everything here is deep-fried. There's grilled Mexican street corn with three different toppings and even a dip with an entire cocktail dumped in it, booze and all.

Recommended portion sizes are just a state of mind – these dips and snacks can all be served as mains if you've got nobody to share with and the right attitude.

Fried pickles

Ingredients

250 ml (8½ fl oz/1 cup) soy milk
1 tablespoon freshly squeezed lemon
    juice or white vinegar
150 g (5½ oz/1 cup) plain (all-purpose) flour
½ teaspoon smoked paprika
60 g (2 oz/1 cup) panko breadcrumbs
sea salt and freshly ground black pepper
canola oil, for deep-frying
120 g (4½ oz) sandwich-stacker dill pickles
    (long sliced gherkins)
dill fronds, to garnish (optional)
Dill cream cheese (see Note on page 168),
    Ranch dipping sauce (see page 167) or
    Tartar sauce (see page 168), to serve

Mother Earth did a pretty good job when it came to cucumbers, and pickles are surely a twist of intelligent design to bring them to their final evolution: sliced and deep-fried until crisp. This recipe takes mere minutes when you purchase sandwich stacker-style pickles to crumb right out of the jar.

Make a basic buttermilk by combining the soy milk and lemon juice or vinegar in a large bowl. Set aside for a few minutes to thicken.

Place the flour and smoked paprika in one bowl and the breadcrumbs in a second bowl. Season both bowls with salt and pepper.

Heat the canola oil in a large heavy-based saucepan over medium–high heat. Test if the oil is ready by inserting a wooden skewer or the handle of a wooden spoon into the oil; if it begins to bubble quickly then you're ready to go.

Fully coat each pickle slice in the flour mixture, followed by the buttermilk and then the breadcrumbs. Make sure each pickle slice is completely coated by using your hands to press the crumbs into the surface and gently shaking off any loose excess.

Fry the pickle slices in small batches for 2–3 minutes, until golden. Transfer to a large plate lined with paper towel to drain and immediately sprinkle with salt.

Scatter over a few dill fronds if you like, and serve with dill cream cheese, ranch dipping sauce, tartar sauce or completely naked.

Mozzarella sticks

Serves 1 heart attack (or more if you share)

Ingredients

200–250 g (7–9 oz) block dairy-free
  cheese
canola oil, for deep-frying
250 ml (8½ fl oz/1 cup) soy milk
1 tablespoon freshly squeezed lemon
  juice or white vinegar
120 g (4½ oz/2 cups) panko breadcrumbs
30 g (1 oz/½ cup) nutritional yeast
75 g (2¾ oz/½ cup) plain (all-purpose) flour
2 teaspoons sea salt
1 teaspoon freshly ground black pepper
tomato ketchup, to serve

Despite the title of this recipe, try to avoid vegan mozzarella alternatives as they usually focus on a melty texture rather than a great cheese flavour. Grab your favourite block of dairy-free cheese with the most cheesy flavour, and it will shine through the crispy crumb it's trapped inside.

Place the cheese in the freezer until you need it. Super-cold cheese is much better for frying.

Heat the canola oil in a large heavy-based saucepan over medium–high heat. Test if the oil is ready by inserting a wooden skewer or the handle of a wooden spoon into the oil; if it begins to bubble quickly then you're ready to go.

Meanwhile, make a basic buttermilk by combining the soy milk and lemon juice or vinegar in a large bowl. Set aside for a few minutes to thicken.

Combine the breadcrumbs and nutritional yeast in one bowl and the flour, salt and pepper in another bowl. Add half the flour mixture to the buttermilk and stir until smooth.

Cut the cheese into eight even-sized sticks. Using a fork, dip each stick into the flour and fully coat before dipping in the buttermilk mixture. Toss in the breadcrumbs and use your hands to press the crumbs into the cheese until fully coated (it's important that all the cheese is covered in breadcrumbs, as most vegan cheeses are oil-based and will disintegrate if they come into direct contact with hot oil).

Working in two batches, add the cheese sticks to the hot oil and fry for a maximum of 2 minutes, taking care not to overcook them and removing as soon as they crisp up.

Drain the cheese sticks on a plate lined with paper towel, before serving warm with ketchup.

Onion rings

Ingredients

250 ml (8½ fl oz/1 cup) soy milk
1 tablespoon freshly squeezed lemon
    juice or white vinegar
2 teaspoons Tabasco sauce (optional)
150 g (5½ oz/1 cup) plain (all-purpose) flour
sea salt and freshly ground black pepper
100 g (3½ oz/1 cup) dried breadcrumbs
canola oil, for deep-frying
1 large onion, sliced into 1–2 cm (½–¾ in)
    thick rings (don't slice them too thinly!)
your favourite dipping sauce, to serve

You can't start crying while chopping onions if you're already crying. Before you feel too sorry for yourself, though, spare a thought for the poor onion: its potent flavour is its natural defence mechanism against predators, which is a fat lot of help seeing as that's exactly why we continue to harvest them. Honour their sacrifice and make sure they end up as a crispy, delicious onion ring.

Make a basic buttermilk by combining the soy milk and lemon juice or vinegar in a large bowl. Set aside for a few minutes to thicken. This is also your cue to add Tabasco if you're using it.

Place the flour in a bowl and season with salt and pepper. Get out one more bowl and tip in the breadcrumbs.

Heat the canola oil in a large heavy-based saucepan over medium–high heat. Test if the oil is ready by inserting a wooden skewer or the handle of a wooden spoon into the oil; if it begins to bubble quickly then you're ready to go.

Separate the onion rings and toss in the seasoned flour. Remove the onion rings and pour the rest of the flour into the buttermilk, stirring until smooth. Dip each ring into the buttermilk batter until fully coated, then lightly press into the breadcrumbs. Fully cover, then shake off any excess.

Lower the rings into the hot oil and fry for 2 minutes, flipping halfway through. Transfer to a large plate lined with paper towel to drain and immediately sprinkle with salt.

Serve with your favourite dipping sauce.

Buffalo cauliflower dip

Ingredients

1 small–medium cauliflower, broken into small florets

1 small onion, thinly sliced

2 tablespoons olive oil

180 g (6½ oz/¾ cup) Cream cheese (see page 169)

1½ teaspoons dried dill

1 tablespoon freshly squeezed lemon juice

½ teaspoon garlic powder

135 g (5 oz/½ cup) Mayonnaise (see page 165 or use store-bought vegan mayonnaise)

185 g (6½ oz/1½ cups) shredded dairy-free cheese

250 ml (8½ fl oz/1 cup) wing sauce, such as Frank's RedHot

50 g (1¾ oz) dairy-free blue cheese (optional)

celery batons, to serve

crackers, to serve

When done right, buffalo cauliflower wings are so spicy it's a public health hazard to serve them without a fire extinguisher on hand in the form of a cooling dip. In the interests of safety, this recipe bakes the whole lot together. You'll break a sweat just making eye contact with this beast as it leaves the oven as a bowl of bubbling goo. Serve with celery batons in a feeble attempt to work in some nutritional content.

Preheat the oven to 200°C (400°F). Line a baking tray with baking paper.

Combine the cauliflower, onion and olive oil in a bowl, then spread out in a single layer on the prepared tray. Bake for 25–30 minutes, until the edges of the cauliflower begin to char. Remove from the oven and reduce the temperature to 175°C (345°F).

In a large bowl, combine the cream cheese, dill, lemon juice, garlic powder, mayonnaise, two-thirds of the shredded cheese and three-quarters of the wing sauce. Add the charred cauliflower and onion, stir well to coat in the cheesy sauce, then transfer to a small baking dish. Pour the remaining wing sauce over the top and sprinkle over the remaining shredded cheese. Bake for 25–30 minutes, until the cheese is bubbling.

Break the blue cheese (if using) into small blobs and position them artistically over the top of the cheesy cauliflower. Serve with celery batons for dipping, then break open that packet of crackers at the back of your pantry for when the celery inevitably runs out.

Battered mushroom 'calamari'

Ingredients

300 g (10½ oz) oyster or king oyster
    mushrooms
250 ml (8½ fl oz/1 cup) soy milk
1 tablespoon freshly squeezed lemon juice
    or white vinegar
150 g (5½ oz/1 cup) plain (all-purpose)
    flour or 125 g (4½ oz/1 cup) cornflour
    (corn starch)
sea salt and freshly ground black pepper
canola oil, for deep-frying
lemon wedges, to serve
Tzatziki mayonnaise (see page 166),
    Tartar sauce (see page 168) or Japanese
    mayonnaise (see page 165), to serve

The hardest part of this whole dish is maintaining eye contact while calling it calamari as you serve it up. It's not exactly like calamari, but only because it's way better with perfectly meaty oyster mushrooms and much easier to catch than squid.

Tear any larger oyster mushrooms into bite-sized pieces. If using king oyster mushrooms, use a vegetable peeler to slice the stalks into thin strips.

Make a basic buttermilk by combining the soy milk and lemon juice or vinegar in a large bowl. Set aside for a few minutes to thicken.

In a separate bowl, combine the flour and salt and pepper.

Meanwhile, heat the canola oil in a large heavy-based saucepan over medium–high heat. Test if the oil is ready by inserting a wooden skewer or the handle of a wooden spoon into the oil; if it begins to bubble quickly then you're ready to go.

Dip the mushroom pieces into the buttermilk, then fully coat in the seasoned flour, gently shaking off any excess. If you allow the mushroom to sit between flouring and frying, you'll need to re-flour them, as the moisture from the mushroom will seep into the dry coating.

Working in small batches, fry the mushroom for 2–3 minutes, until just beginning to brown. Transfer to a large plate lined with paper towel to drain and sprinkle with salt.

Serve immediately with lemon wedges, tzatziki mayonnaise, tartar sauce or Japanese mayonnaise.

Deep-fried mac 'n' cheese balls

Ingredients

2 tablespoons olive oil or dairy-free butter
150 g (5½ oz/1 cup) plain (all-purpose) flour
560 ml (19 fl oz/2¼ cups) soy milk, plus
  extra if needed
45 g (1½ oz/¾ cup) nutritional yeast
1 teaspoon garlic powder
1 teaspoon Dijon mustard
185 g (6½ oz/1½ cups) shredded
  dairy-free cheese
250 g (9 oz) dried macaroni, cooked
  according to the packet instructions
125 ml (4 fl oz/½ cup) aquafaba
120 g (4½ oz/2 cups) panko breadcrumbs
2 teaspoons sea salt
1 teaspoon freshly ground black pepper
2 teaspoons dried basil
canola oil, for deep-frying

If you're just after a good bowl of mac 'n' cheese, stir the cooked pasta through the bechamel sauce, divide among bowls and dig in. To make it even better, transfer the mixture to a baking dish, top with the panko breadcrumbs and bake in a preheated 200°C (400°F) oven for up to 30 minutes, until golden. You could also add cooked vegetables if you'd like to make it worse (healthier).

Vegan cheese tends to come in two categories: good at melting or good at tasting good. Whichever you choose, the majority of dairy-free cheese usually benefits from using the back of a spoon to press down halfway through cooking to promote better melting. In this recipe, the deep-frying forgives most vegan cheese sins by ensuring it's melted to a delicious goo by the time it's served.

Heat the olive oil or butter in a large saucepan over medium heat. Sift in 3 tablespoons of the flour and stir constantly for 1–2 minutes, until you have a roux. Once the roux starts to bubble, gradually whisk in the soy milk a little at a time. When all the liquid has been added, reduce the heat to low and let the bechamel simmer, stirring frequently, for several minutes until thickened.

Stir through 15 g (½ oz/¼ cup) of the nutritional yeast, the garlic powder and mustard. If the sauce is very thick, add a splash more soy milk. Stir through the cheese, then simmer for a further 10–15 minutes. You'll know it's done when the sauce comes away from the side of the pan. Be aware that it will continue to thicken once you remove it from the heat. Stir through the cooked pasta, transfer to a large bowl and set aside in the fridge until completely chilled (see Note opposite).

Place the aquafaba and remaining flour in separate shallow bowls. Combine the breadcrumbs, salt, pepper, basil and remaining nutritional yeast in a third shallow bowl.

Using a dessertspoon, scoop out a spoonful of the macaroni cheese and use your hands to roll it into a tight ball. Roll the ball into the flour to coat, then dip in the aquafaba. Allow any excess aquafaba to drip off, then roll in the breadcrumbs and use your hands to press the breadcrumbs into the mac 'n' cheese ball. Shake off any excess breadcrumbs and place on a tray while you make the remaining mac 'n' cheese balls.

Meanwhile, heat the oil in a large heavy-based saucepan over medium–high heat. Test if the oil is ready by inserting a wooden skewer or the handle of a wooden spoon into the oil; if it begins to bubble quickly then you're ready to go.

Working in batches, fry the balls for 2–3 minutes, until crispy and golden. Drain on paper towel, then transfer to a serving plate and serve immediately.

Sausage rolls

Ingredients

olive oil

1 onion, roughly chopped

4 garlic cloves, finely chopped

200 g (7 oz) chestnut or button
  mushrooms, roughly chopped

2 beef- or chicken-style stock cubes

1 tablespoon soy sauce

2 teaspoons vegan Worcestershire sauce

1 teaspoon thyme or rosemary leaves

5 drops liquid smoke (optional)

250 g (9 oz) vegan mince or vegan burger
  patties, broken up into chunks

2 teaspoons Dijon mustard

pinch of freshly ground black pepper

2 tablespoons finely chopped flat-leaf
  parsley leaves

2 sheets dairy-free frozen puff pastry, just
  thawed

2 teaspoons soy milk

1 teaspoon sesame seeds (optional)

1 teaspoon poppy seeds (optional)

tomato ketchup, to serve

My sausage rolls are a consistent crowd pleaser, with mushrooms and herbs serving to bulk out your choice of 'meat' and give off gourmet vibes. The wash of milk and oil somehow makes them simultaneously crispy and soft, and ensures they're just as good days later if your rolls survive long enough to become cold and old.

Preheat the oven to 200°C (400°F).

Heat 1 tablespoon olive oil in a frying pan over medium heat. Add the onion and cook, stirring occasionally, for 5 minutes. Add the garlic and mushroom and continue to cook until the mushroom has broken down and any liquid has evaporated. Transfer the mushroom mixture to a food processor, along with the stock cubes, soy sauce, Worcestershire sauce, thyme or rosemary leaves and the liquid smoke (if using) and blitz to combine.

Place the mince in a large bowl and use a fork to mash the mustard, pepper and parsley into the mince. Stir in the mushroom mixture until well combined. Divide the mixture into quarters.

Cut the pastry sheets in half and place them in front of you. Evenly spoon the mince mixture along the long edge of each pastry sheet, then fold the pastry sheets over to enclose the filling and use a fork to crimp and seal the edges. Press the sausage rolls down on this crease to seal shut, then cut in half and stuff any filling that's fallen out back into the open ends.

Whisk 4 teaspoons olive oil and the soy milk in a small bowl. Using a pastry brush, brush the mixture over the top of each sausage roll and sprinkle with the sesame seeds and/or poppy seeds (if using). Bake for 25–35 minutes, until golden.

Serve with tomato ketchup or your favourite tomato sauce.

The sausage rolls will keep in an airtight container in the fridge for 3–4 days or in the freezer for up to 3 months.

Deep-fried lasagne

Ingredients

shredded dairy-free cheese, for scattering
½ quantity leftover Lasagne (see page 104)
185 ml (6½ fl oz/¾ cup) aquafaba
75 g (2¾ oz/½ cup) plain (all-purpose) flour
120 g (4½ oz/2 cups) panko breadcrumbs
2 teaspoons sea salt
1 teaspoon freshly ground black pepper
canola oil, for deep-frying
leftover lasagne sauce (see page 104) or
    marinara sauce, to serve
basil leaves, to garnish (optional)

We all know lasagne to be one of the heartiest meals around with its layers of meat and tomato sauce, cheesy bechamel and pasta. This rich combination is usually enough for most people, but I say let's take it to the next level and deep-fry it to boot.

Scatter cheese over the leftover lasagne, then refrigerate it overnight. Cut the lasagne into 5.5 cm (2¼ in) squares.

Place the aquafaba, flour and breadcrumbs in three separate shallow bowls. Season the breadcrumbs with the salt and pepper.

Heat the canola oil in a large heavy-based saucepan over medium–high heat.

Take a square of lasagne and coat it in the flour, followed by the aquafaba and finally in the breadcrumb mixture. Use your hands to press as many breadcrumbs into the surface as possible, taking this opportunity to reshape the lasagne if desired: I like to form mine into rough patties by pressing down during this step. Shake any loose breadcrumbs off and make sure none of the extra shredded cheese is peeking out. Set aside on a tray and repeat with the remaining lasagne squares.

Test if the oil is ready by inserting a wooden skewer or the handle of a wooden spoon into the oil; if it begins to bubble quickly then you're ready to go. Working in small batches, add the crumbed lasagne and fry for 1–2 minutes, until golden on all sides.

Using a slotted spoon, transfer the deep-fried lasagne to a large plate lined with paper towel to drain. Allow to cool to room temperature.

Serve with leftover lasagne sauce or marinara sauce for dipping and basil leaves scattered over the top if you like.

Southern-fried cauliflower

Ingredients

375 ml (12½ fl oz/1½ cups) aquafaba
1 cauliflower, chopped into
    bite-sized florets
canola oil, for deep-frying
your favourite dipping sauces, to serve

Southern-fried spice mix

225 g (8 oz/1½ cups) plain
    (all-purpose) flour
1½ tablespoons brown sugar
1 teaspoon sea salt
1 teaspoon smoked paprika
1 teaspoon onion powder
1 teaspoon chilli powder
½ teaspoon garlic powder
½ teaspoon celery salt
½ teaspoon ground sage
½ teaspoon ground allspice
½ teaspoon dried basil
¼ teaspoon dried oregano
1 teaspoon kala namak (Indian black salt)
    or use regular salt
2 teaspoons MSG or torula yeast (optional)

The other, other 'white meat'. Cauliflower takes about the same amount of time to cook as chicken and pairs well with the same flavours so it's a no-brainer substitute. Use up all those leftover florets from the Southern-fried 'chicken' drumsticks on page 94 in this 15-minute dish.

Combine the spice mix ingredients in a large bowl and pour the aquafaba into a separate bowl.

Heat the canola oil in a large heavy-based saucepan over medium–high heat. Test if the oil is ready by inserting a wooden skewer or the handle of a wooden spoon into the oil; if it begins to bubble quickly then you're ready to go.

Dip the cauliflower florets in the aquafaba, then coat in the spice mix, repeating once. If you're not frying the cauliflower immediately, you may need to toss some extra spice mix over the florets to ensure their exterior is dry.

Working in small batches, fry the cauliflower for 3–4 minutes, until golden brown. Transfer the cauliflower to a large plate lined with paper towel to drain.

Serve the Southern-fried cauliflower with your favourite dipping sauces: Mayonnaise (see page 165), Ranch (see page 167), barbecue, chilli, sriracha, buffalo, aioli or whatever's on hand!

Crabless cakes

Ingredients

120 g (4½ oz) salted crackers
2 tomatoes, diced
1 spring onion (scallion), roughly chopped
1 teaspoon Dijon mustard
½ teaspoon Tabasco sauce
½ teaspoon white vinegar
4 teaspoons shredded nori
1 teaspoon vegan Worcestershire sauce
1½ tablespoons Old Bay Seasoning
400 g (14 oz) tin hearts of palm,
    rinsed and drained, halved lengthways
    and sliced
canola oil, for shallow-frying

To serve

tahini
chopped dill fronds
chopped dill pickles (gherkins)
celery salt
lemon wedges

Salted crackers crushed to dust form the base of this recipe. You can easily replace the crackers with ready-made breadcrumbs, but then you don't get the catharsis of assaulting your ingredients first. Your call.

Crush the crackers into a fine dust using either a food processor or in a zip-lock bag with a rolling pin and lots of gusto. Transfer to a large bowl.

Process the tomato, spring onion, mustard, Tabasco, vinegar, nori, Worcestershire sauce and Old Bay Seasoning in the small bowl of a food processer. Stir the mixture through the crushed crackers before mixing in the hearts of palm. Set aside for 15 minutes.

Roll the crabless cake mixture into 12–14 balls and press down lightly to make mini cakes.

Heat 1 cm (½ in) of canola oil in a large frying pan over high heat. Working in batches, add the cakes to the oil, flattening further with a spatula if desired before spooning some hot oil over the top. Cook for about 1½ minutes each side, until crisp and golden brown. Transfer to a plate lined with paper towel to drain.

Swirl some tahini on a serving plate and top with the crabless cakes. Scatter over a few dill fronds, chopped dill pickle and some celery salt, and serve with lemon wedges on the side.

Cashew queso dip

Ingredients

155 g (5½ oz/1 cup) raw cashews
2 carrots, chopped into chunks
170 g (6 oz) potatoes, chopped into chunks
60 ml (2 fl oz/¼ cup) freshly squeezed
    lemon juice
2 teaspoons garlic powder
2 teaspoons onion powder
⅔ teaspoon smoked paprika
1½ teaspoons vegan lactic acid (optional;
    see Note opposite)
2 tablespoons olive oil
35 g (1¼ oz/¼ cup) plain (all-purpose) flour
375 ml (12½ fl oz/1½ cups) soy milk
60 g (2 oz/1 cup) nutritional yeast
250 g (9 oz/2 cups) shredded
    dairy-free cheddar

Salsa

1 tablespoon olive oil
1 small onion, finely chopped
3 large green chillies, finely chopped
400 g (14 oz) tin crushed tomatoes
1 tablespoon white vinegar

Queso dip is the creamy and slightly spicy child of cheese and salsa, and it feels right at home on top of most things that call for cheese sauce. Choose American or cheddar-style dairy-free cheese for a flavour that won't get lost in the salsa and to achieve an unnerving shade of orange. Increase the volume of soaked cashews in the recipe for a thicker dip that needs nothing more than a swirl of extra salsa on top and corn chips to serve.

Soak the cashews overnight in a bowl of cold water. If you don't have time to do this, simply place the cashews in a saucepan and cover with cold water. Bring to the boil over medium–high heat and boil for 15 minutes to soften. Drain and set aside.

Place the carrot and potato in a saucepan and cover with cold water. Bring to the boil, then reduce the heat to medium and simmer for 8–10 minutes, until cooked through. Drain, then return the vegetables to the pan and mash together.

Transfer the mashed vegetables to a high-powered blender or food processor, along with the cashews, lemon juice, garlic and onion powders, paprika and lactic acid (if using), and blend until completely smooth and combined.

To make the salsa, heat the olive oil in a frying pan over medium heat. Sauté the onion for at least 10 minutes, until golden brown. Add the chilli and sauté for a further 2 minutes. Add the tomatoes and vinegar and cook, stirring occasionally, for 10 minutes or until reduced to a chunky salsa.

Meanwhile, heat the olive oil in a saucepan over medium heat until bubbling. Sift in the flour and stir constantly for 1–2 minutes, until you have a roux. Once the roux starts to bubble, gradually whisk in the soy milk a little at a time, allowing each addition of liquid to be absorbed before adding the next. When all the liquid has been added, reduce the heat to low and let the bechamel simmer, stirring frequently, for several minutes until thickened. Stir in the nutritional yeast and cheddar and simmer for a further 10 minutes. It will be quite thick.

Add the bechamel to the blended cashew mixture and blend or process until smooth. Transfer to a large bowl and stir through the salsa adding 3 tablespoons at a time and tasting as you go until you're satisfied with the flavour. Serve as a dip or a sauce by pouring over anything, including your open mouth.

If you're making this dip to serve with the Nachos or Herb-stuffed cheese quesadillas on pages 92 and 125, serve the salsa on the side as a dipping sauce instead of stirring it through the cashew queso.

Vegan lactic acid adds a lovely cheesy flavour to dishes. It is available online.

Bloody Mary 'crab' cob loaf

Ingredients

1.1 kg (2 lb 7 oz) tinned young jackfruit,
 rinsed and drained
220 g (8 oz) Cream cheese (see page 169)
4 teaspoons grated onion, plus extra
 if needed
1 tablespoon Old Bay Seasoning,
 plus extra if needed
2 nori sheets, shredded, plus extra
 if needed
1 large cob loaf

Bloody Mary

160 ml (5½ fl oz) vodka or tequila
500 ml (17 fl oz/2 cups) tomato juice
1 tablespoon vegan Worcestershire sauce
1 teaspoon Tabasco sauce
2 teaspoons pickle juice from a dill pickle
 (gherkin) jar (optional)
2 tablespoons finely chopped pickled
 jalapeno chillies
freshly ground black pepper, to taste
2 teaspoons capers, rinsed and drained

To serve

celery stalks
skewered cherry tomatoes, pickles
 and olives

If you look into a mirror and say Bloody Mary three times nobody will appear, but you might start thinking about brunch. It doesn't matter what time you start drinking when you've already mixed an entire cocktail into this dish. This cob loaf makes enough for a very festive party or one lonely host if nobody comes.

Take your jackfruit pieces and cut away the hard core. Squeeze each piece so that any seeds pop out and any excess liquid is removed, then gently pull the jackfruit pieces to make them stringy. This will be our 'crab meat'.

Preheat the oven to 180°C (350°F). Line a baking tray with baking paper.

To make the bloody Mary, combine your booze of choice with the tomato juice, Worcestershire sauce, Tabasco, pickle juice (if using), jalapeno, pepper and capers in a saucepan. Add the jackfruit, then immediately make yourself another bloody Mary (this one is optional and exclusively for drinking). Place the pan over medium heat and simmer for 10–15 minutes, until most of the liquid has evaporated. Transfer the mixture to a bowl and set aside to cool for 10 minutes.

Add the cream cheese, onion, Old Bay Seasoning and nori to the jackfruit mixture and mix well. Check the seasoning and adjust with more onion, Old Bay and/or nori if necessary.

Use a serrated knife to remove the top of the cob loaf and pluck out most of the bread inside. Fill the hollowed-out loaf with the 'crab' dip and place the bread lid back on top. Wrap the cob loaf in foil.

Transfer the cob loaf to the prepared tray and bake for 30 minutes. Remove the loaf from the oven and carefully remove the foil. Place the cob loaf back on the baking tray and scatter the bread pieces around the loaf. Return to the oven and bake until the loaf and bread pieces begin to crisp.

Serve warm with the bread for dipping, along with celery stalks and skewered cherry tomatoes, pickles and olives or anything else you'd usually pair with a bloody Mary.

Reward yourself with another bloody Mary.

Fried green tomatoes

Ingredients

250 ml (8½ fl oz/1 cup) soy milk
1 tablespoon freshly squeezed lemon
 juice or white vinegar
a hearty amount of Tabasco sauce
pinch of kala namak (Indian black salt;
 optional)
4–6 green tomatoes, cut into 2 cm
 (¾ in) thick slices
sea salt
110 g (4 oz/¾ cup) polenta or cornmeal
45 g (1½ oz/¾ cup) panko breadcrumbs
freshly ground black pepper
50 g (1¾ oz/⅓ cup) plain (all-purpose) flour
pinch of Cajun seasoning (optional)
canola oil, for deep-frying
freshly snipped chives, to garnish
Ranch dipping sauce (see page 167),
 to serve

You can easily whip up a batch of Fried pickles (see page 18) while making this dish, so you have a bonus-round meal ready for when you've eaten the last crumbs on the plate and are looking for something to mop up the extra ranch sauce. Or get ahead of the game and make a double batch of fried green tomatoes in the first place.

Make a basic buttermilk by combining the soy milk and lemon juice or vinegar in a large bowl. Set aside for a few minutes to thicken. Add a few good dashes of Tabasco and the kala namak (if using).

Discard the top and bottom slices of the tomato and place the remaining slices on a large plate. Season the tomato with salt and set aside for a few minutes, then soak in the buttermilk for 10 minutes.

If using polenta, run it through a food processor for several seconds until finely milled. Transfer the polenta or cornmeal to a bowl and stir through the breadcrumbs. Season with salt and pepper. Place the flour and Cajun seasoning (if using) in a separate bowl.

Heat the canola oil in a large heavy-based saucepan over medium–high heat. Test if the oil is ready by inserting a wooden skewer or the handle of a wooden spoon into the oil; if it begins to bubble quickly then you're ready to go.

Use a fork to lift a tomato slice out of the buttermilk. Allow a little of the buttermilk to drip, but don't shake off the excess. Coat the tomato in the flour, then return to the buttermilk and gently coat each side before coating in the breadcrumb mixture. Press the crumbs into the surface of the tomato with your hands and shake off any loose excess. Repeat with the remaining tomato slices.

Working in small batches, fry the tomato for 4–6 minutes (larger slices may take a minute longer), until crisp. The tomato tends to float to the surface of the oil, so flip them around as needed to crisp up both sides. Transfer to a large plate lined with paper towel to drain.

Garnish the fried green tomatoes with chives and serve warm with a bowl of ranch dipping sauce on the side.

Poutine

Ingredients

canola oil, for deep-frying
1–1.2 kg (2 lb 3 oz–2 lb 10 oz) frozen fries
60 g (2 oz) dairy-free butter
40 g (1½ oz) plain (all-purpose) flour
4 teaspoons beef-style stock powder
500 ml (17 fl oz/2 cups) hot water, plus extra if needed
1 tablespoon dark soy sauce
2 teaspoons balsamic vinegar
1 teaspoon Vegemite
1 teaspoon freshly ground black pepper
sea salt
185 g (6½ oz/1½ cups) shredded or soft dairy-free cheese

There are few foods as celebrated as the potato. For example, fries are the finest vegan offering available at many of the world's top restaurants. Let's elevate that dish the Canadian way with hot gravy and melted cheese.

Heat the canola oil in a large saucepan over medium–high heat. Test if the oil is ready by inserting a wooden skewer or the handle of a wooden spoon into the oil; if it begins to bubble quickly then you're ready to go.

Working in two batches, fry the fries until they're extra crispy. This can take 10 plus minutes, but it's important as we want them to be as crunchy as possible to stand up against the wave of gravy coming their way.

While the fries are frying, prepare the gravy. Heat the butter in a small saucepan over medium heat until bubbling. Sift in the flour and stir constantly for 1–2 minutes, until you have a roux, then stir through the stock powder. Slowly add the water while stirring to create a gravy base. Add the soy sauce, vinegar and Vegemite and simmer for 5–10 minutes, until thickened. You can add more water if you would like a thinner gravy. Taste and add the pepper (don't skip it as it makes a great difference).

Place a few paper towels in a large serving dish and transfer the chips to the dish once they are crisp. Whip out the paper towel and immediately and aggressively salt the fries and toss to distribute. If using a soft cheese, tear it into small blobs. Add the cheese to the fries and toss again.

Pour the gravy over the top and stir to distribute. You may like to cover the dish in foil for a few minutes to help the cheese melt.

Eat while the fries are still hot and crisp.

Jalapeno poppers

Ingredients

6 fresh jalapeno chillies

125 ml (4 fl oz/½ cup) soy milk

2 teaspoons freshly squeezed lemon juice
or white vinegar

60 g (2 oz/1 cup) panko breadcrumbs

30 g (1 oz/½ cup) nutritional yeast

75 g (2¾ oz/½ cup) plain (all-purpose) flour

2 teaspoons sea salt

1 teaspoon freshly ground black pepper

90 g (3 oz/⅓ cup) Cream cheese
(see page 169) mixed with 1 minced
garlic clove

30 g (1 oz/¼ cup) shredded dairy-free
cheddar

canola oil, for deep-frying

When I die, I hope to be reincarnated as a jalapeno popper so I know what it feels like to be flawless in every way. Crispy and spicy on the outside with cooling cream cheese in the centre to balance it all out, this combination gives you your best chance at persevering through an entire bowl of chillies without needing any help from your friends.

Use a sharp paring knife to cut a T shape into the flesh of one side of each jalapeno. The aim is to keep the stem and body of the chilli intact, so make the first incision just under the stem, only cutting halfway through the chilli. Intersect this incision with another cut along the length of the chilli.

Bring a small saucepan of water to the boil over high heat. Use a small teaspoon to prise open the jalapenos and scrape out the chilli seeds and membranes, while keeping the chillies intact. Reserve the seeds and discard the membranes. Drop each chilli into the boiling water and blanch for 3 minutes, then drain and rinse under cold running water to stop the cooking process.

Make a basic buttermilk by combining the soy milk and lemon juice or vinegar in a tall glass. Set aside for a few minutes to thicken.

Combine the breadcrumbs and nutritional yeast in one bowl and the flour, salt and pepper in another bowl.

Mix the cream cheese with the shredded cheese and, if you can handle it, stir through some of the scraped jalapeno seeds. Use a teaspoon to scoop 2 tablespoons of the cream cheese mixture into each hollowed-out jalapeno. The cheese mixture will help the jalapeno poppers seal shut.

Heat the canola oil in a large heavy-based saucepan over medium–high heat. Test if the oil is ready by inserting a wooden skewer or the handle of a wooden spoon into the oil; if it begins to bubble quickly then you're ready to go.

Picking up a popper by its stem, coat it in the seasoned flour, then dip into the tall glass, swirling to fully coat the chilli in the buttermilk. Finally, roll the popper in the breadcrumbs until completely coated. Repeat with the remaining poppers.

Working in batches, fry the poppers in the hot oil for 3 minutes or until crisp and golden. Transfer to paper towel to drain.

Serve hot and don't waste time fiddling with dipping sauces as these poppers are the whole package.

Mexican street corn

Ingredients

4 large sweetcorn cobs, husks and silks
    removed
vegetable oil, if needed
coriander (cilantro) sprigs, to garnish
    (optional)

Simple

dairy-free butter, melted
nutritional yeast, for sprinkling

Chilli–lime

2½ tablespoons chilli powder
zest of 2 limes, plus lime wedges to serve
1 teaspoon citric acid
2 teaspoons sumac
2 teaspoons granulated sugar
1 teaspoon sea salt
115 g (4 oz) Mayonnaise (see page 165 or
    use store-bought vegan mayonnaise)

Jalapeno–mustard

60 g (2 oz/¼ cup) Dijon mustard
2 tablespoons finely chopped pickled
    jalapeno chillies
1½ teaspoons onion powder
1½ teaspoons dried chives
1 teaspoon smoked paprika
½ teaspoon ground ginger
nutritional yeast, for sprinkling
lime wedges, to serve

Known as 'elote' in Mexico, this dish comes with three toppings that all take minutes to prepare, so by the time the corn has grilled you can pick which one to slather on first. Keep any left-over chilli–lime spice or jalapeno–mustard and apply liberally to everything you can.

Place a chargrill pan over high heat and add the corn. Add a few splashes of water to help the corn steam, then cook, adding vegetable oil if the corn starts to stick and turning occasionally, for 20 minutes or until charred on all sides.

Meanwhile prepare your chosen toppings. To make the simple topping, dip the cooked corn in melted butter, then generously sprinkle with nutritional yeast.

To make the chilli–lime topping, combine the ingredients except the mayonnaise in a bowl. Alternatively, if you have the Mexican seasoning Tajin in your pantry, use that instead. It's much easier! Spread 2 tablespoons of mayonnaise over the surface of each cooked corn and sprinkle the spice mix over the top. Serve with lime wedges for squeezing over.

To make the jalapeno–mustard topping, combine the mustard, jalapeno, onion powder, dried chives, paprika and ginger in a bowl. Liberally brush the corn with the mustard mixture to completely coat, sprinkle with nutritional yeast and serve with lime wedges.

Garnish the corn with coriander sprigs, if you like.

SANDWICHES, BURGERS AND DOGS

If someone was to browse the plant-based section at the supermarket, they'd be forgiven for assuming the vegan diet is primarily made up of burger patties. There was a brief moment in time when burgers were a wild fantasy for vegans, but now we can have them every which way, every day.

The following pages are a global adventure centred around bread. Make impossibly soft buns for bao or unceremoniously scoop smoky seitan, capsicum (bell pepper), shallots and cheese into crusty bread for a Philly faux-steak. Alternatively, replace the bread altogether in a Korean hot dog with a crust made from crinkle-cut fries. Hamburgers are also in plentiful supply, whether they're filled with bhajis, built for breakfast or presented in the burger form of a behemoth, aka the big Zac.

Breakfast burritos

Ingredients

400 g (14 oz) firm tofu
1 tablespoon olive oil
½ teaspoon ground cumin
1 teaspoon kala namak (Indian black salt)
1¼ tablespoons dairy-free butter or
    olive oil
2 tablespoons chickpea flour (besan)
310 ml (10½ fl oz/1¼ cups) soy milk
15 g (½ oz/¼ cup) nutritional yeast
60 g (2 oz/½ cup) shredded
    dairy-free cheese
½ teaspoon Dijon mustard
4 large wheat tortillas
400 g (14 oz) tin black beans, drained
    and rinsed
freshly ground black papper
hot sauce, for drizzling (optional)
2 avocados

Pico de gallo

2 tomatoes, finely chopped
½ red onion, finely chopped
1–2 fresh jalapeno chillies or 1 long green
    chilli, finely chopped
½ bunch coriander (cilantro), leaves
    picked and finely chopped, plus extra
    leaves to serve
juice of ½ lime, plus lime wedges to serve
sea salt and freshly ground black pepper

"Where do you get your protein from?" is a question posed to vegans globally by people who have seemingly yet to discover the concept of supermarkets. Protein is abundant in plants, but for those who are still concerned there's this breakfast burrito with an array of protein sources, such as tofu, chickpea flour (besan), black beans and wheat tortillas all bundled up with fresh salsa and avocado.

Squeeze the liquid out of the tofu, then break it into large chunks.

Heat the olive oil in a frying pan over medium heat, add the tofu and brown for 10 minutes on as many sides as you can. Add the cumin and three-quarters of the kala namak and cook until fragrant (or stinking, depending on what you think of the smell of egg). Remove from the heat and set aside.

Heat the butter or oil in a small saucepan over medium heat until bubbling. Gradually stir in the chickpea flour for 1–2 minutes, until you have a roux. Once the roux starts to bubble, gradually whisk in the soy milk a little at a time. Mix in the nutritional yeast, cheese and mustard. Add the braised tofu chunks, stir and allow the sauce to thicken for a few minutes and cling to the tofu.

Preheat the oven to 160°C (320°F).

To make the pico de gallo, combine the tomato, onion, chilli and coriander in a small bowl. Stir through the lime juice and season with salt and pepper.

Lay out four large squares of foil and place a tortilla on top of each square.

Divide the black beans and tofu mixture among the tortillas, sprinkling the remaining black salt and a little pepper over the top. Spoon over the pico de gallo and drizzle with hot sauce if that's what you're into, then use the foil to wrap everything up into a snug burrito. Twist the ends of the foil to seal, then transfer to the oven and bake for 15–20 minutes, until warmed through.

When the burritos are ready, dice the avocados or mash them in a bowl. Unwrap the burritos and add all the avocado only to your burrito. Serve everyone else's without or, if they catch you, share the avocado among the burritos along with a few coriander leaves. Serve with lime wedges on the side.

'Egg' and 'bacon' muffins

Ingredients

600 g (1 lb 5 oz) silken tofu
canola oil, for shallow-frying
30 g (1 oz/¼ cup) cornflour (corn starch)
freshly ground black pepper
kala namak (Indian black salt)
2 slices dairy-free cheddar
dairy-free butter, for spreading
2 vegan English muffins, sliced in half
3 sheets chewy Rice paper bacon
   (see page 164), cut into 'rashers'
Dijon or American mustard,
   for spreading (optional)

Kala namak smells and tastes an awful lot like egg and I do mean awful – it stinks! Used sparingly, it can turn your egg-style dishes into deceivingly good substitutes; used excessively it can be militarised as a chemical weapon.

Drain the silken tofu and freeze until needed. You don't want to let it completely freeze, but firming it up in the freezer will make it easier to manage.

Heat enough canola oil for shallow-frying in a heavy-based frying pan over medium heat.

Slice the tofu block into quarters to roughly match the size of the English muffins. Alternatively, slide an egg ring through the tofu and slice the resulting tube into four rings.

Combine the cornflour and ½ teaspoon each of pepper and kala namak in a bowl. Very gently add the tofu slices and coat in the flour mixture – the water content in the tofu is a form of aquafaba and this will help the flour to stick.

Immediately add the floured tofu pieces to the hot oil and fry, flipping once, for 5 minutes or until both sides are crisp and brown. Transfer to a plate lined with paper towel and sprinkle over an extra pinch of pepper and kala namak.

Remove most of the oil from the pan. Add the cheese slices and cook for a few seconds before immediately removing with a spatula and placing on top of the fried tofu.

Smear a blob of butter over the cut sides of the English muffins and fry, buttered side down, until lightly toasted.

Stack a few pieces of rice paper bacon on two muffin halves, followed by a piece of cheesy, fried tofu. You can stop there, but you shouldn't, so add more bacon and another piece of cheesy fried tofu. Smear some mustard on the remaining muffin halves if you like, then close up and devour while still warm.

Lox and schmear bagels

Ingredients

6 firm, slightly under-ripe tomatoes
4 nori sheets, shredded
125 ml (4 fl oz/½ cup) soy sauce
1 tablespoon ground ginger
1 teaspoon liquid smoke
4 bagels, sliced in half
250 g (9 oz/1 cup) Dill cream cheese
   (see Note on page 168)
1 red onion, thinly sliced
2 tablespoons capers, rinsed and drained
dill fronds, to garnish (optional)

Liquid smoke isn't a scary ingredient, it's simply smoke passed through water to enable you to trick your friends into thinking you've spent hours lovingly cooking a dish for them. When used to marinate tomatoes, they become reminiscent of smoked salmon.

Score a shallow cross into the top of each tomato. Bring a saucepan of water to the boil over medium–high heat, add the tomatoes and boil for no more than 1 minute. Drain and plunge the tomatoes into a bowl of ice-cold water. This means you can easily remove the skins while keeping the raw tomato texture we want for this dish.

Cut each tomato into eight wedges. Use your fingers to remove and discard the seeds and squeeze out any liquid, leaving only the core and firm flesh. If desired, slice these pieces even more thinly to replicate the thickness of smoked salmon. Pat dry with paper towel.

Place the nori in a small bowl of hot water for 1 minute to hydrate. Drain, then place in a large bowl with the soy sauce, ginger, liquid smoke and tomato. Set aside in the fridge to marinate for at least 1 hour or until required.

Toast the bagels, then smear 2 tablespoons of dill cream cheese on each toasted bagel half. Top with the marinated tomato, red onion and capers, then garnish with a few dill fronds (if using). Serve warm.

Philly faux-steak

Ingredients

1 red capsicum (bell pepper), thinly sliced

4 shallots, thinly sliced

sea salt and freshly ground black pepper

olive oil

splash of white vinegar

400 g (14 oz) shredded seitan, frozen
until solid

4 long crusty rolls (hoagie rolls)

dairy-free butter, for spreading

Mayonnaise (see page 165 or use
store-bought vegan mayonnaise), for
spreading

1 tablespoon liquid smoke

1½ tablespoons light soy sauce

120 ml (4 fl oz) Cashew queso dip (see
page 38; omit the salsa) or 240 g (8½ oz)
soft dairy-free cheese

Grease is the word, so you'll want to splash plenty of oil in the pan when making this sandwich, to soak up the rich umami flavour of the seitan, the smoke from the charring capsicum and the sweetness from the caramelised onions. Uncomplicated, yet nearly impossible to improve on. It's the one that you want.

Heat a large frying pan over medium–high heat, add the capsicum and sauté for 5 minutes, then add the shallot. Liberally crack some salt and pepper into the pan and add 2 tablespoons of olive oil. Caramelise the capsicum and shallot for 10 minutes, splashing a little water into the pan now and then and frequently scraping up any bits that catch on the base of the pan. Reduce the heat to low and caramelise for a further 10 minutes.

Splash the vinegar into the pan, then scrape everything into a bowl. Cover with foil and set aside to allow the capsicum to continue to steam and soften. Wipe out the frying pan.

Defrost the seitan for 1 hour, then use a bread knife to shave it into thin strips. Set aside to finish defrosting.

Heat the frying pan again over medium heat. Use the bread knife to cut the rolls almost in half, leaving them still attached on one side, then generously butter the insides and place, buttered side down, in the hot pan, pressing down with a spatula. Once toasted, flip the rolls over and toast for 30 seconds to warm through. Transfer the rolls to plates and spread mayonnaise over the melted butter.

Add another splash of oil to the pan and increase the heat to high. When sizzling, add the seitan and use two forks to shred the 'meat'. Continue to cook for about 10 minutes, until the seitan is crisp and starting to char at the edges. Stir in the liquid smoke and soy sauce, then reduce the heat to low and season to taste with salt and pepper. Toss the capsicum and shallot back into the pan and mix everything together.

In the pan, divide the seitan mixture into quarters. Pour 2 tablespoons of cheese sauce over each portion or divide the soft cheese among the portions and allow it to warm through.

Working with one roll at a time, lay an open roll over a portion of seitan mixture and use a spatula to shimmy the mixture into the roll. Squeeze the roll shut and use the spatula to scrape up any pieces you might have missed and force them into the roll, too.

Mitraillette

Ingredients

1.5 kg (3 lb 5 oz) large russet potatoes
sea salt
canola oil, for deep-frying
600 g (1 lb 5 oz) any processed faux
    meat of your choice
seasoned salt, such as vegan chicken salt
4 small baguettes
dairy-free butter, for spreading

Andalouse sauce

1 x quantity Mayonnaise (see page 165 or
    use store-bought vegan mayonnaise)
2½ tablespoons finely chopped roasted
    red capsicum (bell pepper)
1½ tablespoons tomato paste
    (concentrated purée)
1 tablespoon very finely chopped
    red onion
1 tablespoon freshly squeezed lemon juice
⅓ teaspoon garlic powder
sea salt and freshly ground black pepper

Mitraillette is to sub sandwiches what a submachine gun is to pistols. Absolute overkill. This classic Belgian sandwich is so overloaded that it's an attack on your health status. The first clue comes from the fact that the word 'mitraillette' directly translates to submachine gun. Secure your helmets before proceeding!

Fill a large saucepan with cold water. Leaving the skins on, slice your potatoes lengthways, then slice into your desired chip thickness. Add the chips to the water as you go, replacing with fresh cold water when done. Soak for at least 4 hours.

Drain the chips and place them back in the pan, cover with fresh cold water and season generously with salt as though you're preparing pasta.

Place the pan over high heat and bring to the boil. Cook the chips until they are soft enough to pierce (the goal is to walk the line of how close you can get them to being cooked through, but without having them actually falling apart). Drain the chips into a colander, then dry completely using a clean tea towel or paper towel. Transfer the dry chips to the freezer to fully cool and firm back up.

Heat the canola oil in a large heavy-based saucepan over medium–high heat to 150°C (300°F). This recipe works with fiddly temperatures so it's best to grab a kitchen thermometer before proceeding.

Working in batches, add the chips to the hot oil, turning the heat to high just after they enter the pan. Loosen the chips with a slotted spoon so they don't stick together. Fry the chips for 8–10 minutes, until they form a light crust. Remove the chips from the oil and drain on a plate lined with paper towel. When dry, return the chips to the freezer to cool, ideally overnight. This can be done in advance. Keep the oil in the pan.

To make the Andalouse sauce, combine the ingredients in a small bowl, then set aside in the fridge for 2–3 hours to allow the flavours to develop.

Cook your faux meat in a frying pan according to the packet instructions. If necessary, break the meat into large chunks to fit in your sandwich towards the end of the cooking process. Transfer the faux meat to a plate, but keep the pan handy as we'll use it again soon.

Reheat the oil to 190°C (375°F). Working in small batches again, fry the chips for 5 minutes or until golden and crisp. If you've got a few dodgy smaller chips, add them a few minutes in so everything crisps up together.

Place a few paper towels into a large bowl and transfer the chips to the bowl as they crisp. When done, whip out the paper towel and discard. Immediately throw an obscene amount of seasoned salt over the chips and toss everything in the bowl.

Heat the frying pan again over medium heat. Use a bread knife to halve the baguettes lengthways. Generously butter the insides and place, buttered side down, in the hot pan, pressing down. Allow to toast for 2 minutes, then transfer the baguettes to serving plates.

Place the faux meat on the bottom half of each roll and top with as many chips as they can architecturally handle. You may be tempted to add some sort of vegetable to balance this out but do not falter. There is no room for nutritional value in this sandwich. Smother the whole thing in the Andalouse sauce and top with the other half of the baguette. Prepare a defibrillator and serve.

Mushroom po'boys

Ingredients

300 g (10½ oz) oyster mushrooms or king
  oyster mushrooms
250 ml (8½ fl oz/1 cup) soy milk
1 tablespoon freshly squeezed lemon juice
  or white vinegar
150 g (5½ oz/1 cup) plain (all-purpose)
  flour or 125 g (4½ oz/1 cup) cornflour
  (corn starch)
sea salt and freshly ground black pepper
canola oil, for deep-frying
Old Bay Seasoning (optional)
2 baby cos (romaine) or gem lettuces,
  leaves separated
2 tomatoes, thinly sliced
4 long crispy rolls, sliced open
1 nori sheet, cut into 4 strips
200 g (7 oz/¾ cup) Tartar sauce
  (see page 168)

The addition of tartar sauce, a sneaky sheet of nori and a pinch of Old Bay Seasoning makes this fried mushroom sandwich tell your taste buds it's enjoying a fried seafood sandwich. You won't miss the real seafood and they won't miss you either.

Tear any larger oyster mushrooms into bite-sized pieces. If using king oyster mushrooms, slice them into thin strips. Place the mushroom in a large bowl.

Make a basic buttermilk by combining the soy milk and lemon juice or vinegar in a large bowl. Set aside for a few minutes to thicken.

Place the flour in a small bowl and stir in a hearty crack of salt and pepper.

Meanwhile, heat the canola oil in a large heavy-based saucepan over medium–high heat. Test if the oil is ready by inserting a wooden skewer or the handle of a wooden spoon into the oil; if it begins to bubble quickly then you're ready to go.

Dip each mushroom piece into the buttermilk, then coat in the seasoned flour, gently shaking off any excess. If you allow the mushroom to sit between flouring and frying, you'll need to re-flour them, as the moisture from the mushroom will seep into the dry coating.

Fry the mushroom in small batches for 2–3 minutes, until golden brown, then transfer to a large plate lined with paper towel to drain. Season immediately with salt and some Old Bay Seasoning if you have it to hand.

Place the lettuce and tomato on the bottom half of each roll and top with the fried mushroom. Place the nori strips on the other cut side of the rolls and generously spread the tartar sauce over the nori.

Close the roll halves together and serve immediately.

Katsu sandos

Ingredients

1 large eggplant (aubergine) OR
   3 × 565 g (1 lb 4 oz) tins young green
   jackfruit, rinsed and drained
560 ml (19 fl oz/2¼ cups)
   chicken-style stock
1 tablespoon nutritional yeast
1½ teaspoons onion powder
15 drops liquid smoke
75 g (2¾ oz/½ cup) plain (all-purpose) flour
2 teaspoons sea salt
1 teaspoon freshly ground black pepper
185 ml (6½ fl oz/¾ cup) aquafaba
120 g (4 oz/2 cups) panko breadcrumbs
canola oil, for shallow-frying
8 slices fancy Japanese soft white bread
dairy-free butter
your favourite mustard, for spreading
75 g (2½ oz/1 cup) shredded
   white cabbage
1 tablespoon rice wine vinegar

Katsu sauce

170 ml (5½ fl oz/⅔ cup) tomato ketchup
90 ml (3 fl oz) vegan Worcestershire sauce
2 tablespoons malt vinegar
2 teaspoons granulated sugar
2 teaspoons mustard powder
1 teaspoon garlic powder
1 teaspoon onion powder

Opt for the softest, fluffiest thick-cut white bread for these sandwiches. If you're out to impress, you'll want to make the jackfruit filling for strangely meaty results. Go for the simpler eggplant version if you just haven't got the time but need this on a regular basis (spoiler: you will).

If making eggplant katsu sandos, peel the eggplant, then cut lengthways into four 2 cm (¾ in) thick slices. Liberally sprinkle salt over the eggplant, then wrap the slices in paper towel and place a heavy object on top for 20 minutes to squeeze out the moisture. Remove the paper towel and wipe off the salt.

If making the more chicken-like jackfruit sando, take your jackfruit pieces and cut away the hard core. Squeeze each piece so that any seeds pop out and any excess liquid is removed, then gently pull the jackfruit pieces to make them stringy. Place the jackfruit in a saucepan with the stock, nutritional yeast, onion powder and liquid smoke. Bring to the boil over medium–high heat, then continue to boil for 10 minutes. Reduce the heat to low and cook for a further 10 minutes or until the liquid is absorbed. Remove from the heat and set aside to cool.

Divide the jackfruit mixture into quarters and wrap each portion in plastic wrap, then fashion into the shape of a chicken fillet. Stow these in the freezer for at least 1½ hours before proceeding.

Meanwhile, combine the katsu sauce ingredients in a small bowl.

Place the flour, salt and pepper in a shallow bowl, the aquafaba in another bowl and the breadcrumbs in a third. Unwrap the chilled jackfruit or take your eggplant slices and coat in the seasoned flour. Dip into the aquafaba and then press into the breadcrumbs, using your fingers to firmly adhere the crumbs to the jackfruit fillets or eggplant slices. Gently shake off any excess.

Heat the canola oil in a large frying pan over medium–high heat. Test if the oil is ready by inserting a wooden skewer or the handle of a wooden spoon into the oil; if it begins to bubble quickly then you're ready to go.

Place the jackfruit fillets or eggplant slices into the oil and fry until golden and crisp. Drain on a plate lined with paper towel.

Spread half the bread slices with butter followed by a smear of mustard. Toss the cabbage with the rice wine vinegar and divide among the four buttered slices. Top with the fried jackfruit fillets or eggplant and a generous amount of katsu sauce. Cap with the remaining bread slices, then halve each sandwich and eat!

Bao!

Ingredients

4 Chinese eggplants or two regular
    eggplants (aubergines)
300 g (10½ oz) firm tofu
2⅓ tablespoons chilli paste, such as
    gochujang, plus extra to serve
2 tablespoons dark soy sauce
2 teaspoons minced garlic
1½ teaspoons maple syrup
1 teaspoon Chinese five-spice powder
1 tablespoon canola oil
1 bunch coriander (cilantro), leaves picked
3 tablespoons fried shallots

Bao

1 × 7 g (¼ oz) packet instant dried yeast
125 ml (4 fl oz/½ cup) warm water
470 g (1 lb 1 oz) plain (all-purpose) flour,
    plus extra for dusting
¾ teaspoon baking powder
2½ tablespoons caster (superfine) sugar
½ teaspoon sea salt
2 tablespoons neutral-flavoured oil, plus
    extra for greasing
125 ml (4 fl oz/½ cup) soy milk

Pickled veg

½ red cabbage, shredded
4 carrots, julienned
375 ml (12½ fl oz/1½ cups) rice wine
    vinegar
50 g (1¾ oz) granulated sugar
2 teaspoons sea salt
2 teaspoons minced ginger

Smoky and spicy eggplant, crumbled tofu, pickled vegetables and pops of crunch and freshness nestled in steamed clouds of dough. This recipe makes buns so soft you'll make anyone bao down.

To make the bao, combine the yeast and warm water in a jug. Set aside for a few minutes, then add a pinch of flour. Once the yeast froths up, it's ready to go.

Combine the flour, baking powder, sugar and salt in a large bowl and make a well in the centre. Whisk the oil and milk into the yeast mixture, then pour into the well. Gently stir to combine until the yeast mixture is completely incorporated, then form into a loose dough.

Transfer the dough to a floured work surface and knead for 5 minutes or until the dough is smooth and elastic. It's ready when you press down on the dough and it springs back. Place into a lightly oiled bowl, cover with a tea towel and leave for 1½ hours or until doubled in size.

Preheat a barbecue grill to high.

To make the pickled veg, place the cabbage and carrot in a bowl. Place the vinegar, sugar, salt and 250 ml (8½ fl oz/1 cup) water in a saucepan and bring to the boil. Once the sugar has dissolved, remove from the heat and pour the vinegar mixture over the veg, then stir through the minced ginger. Set aside for at least 1 hour.

Pierce the eggplants a few times with a fork, then place directly on the barbecue grill and cook, rotating frequently, for 15 minutes or until completely blackened and collapsed. Transfer to a plate.

Use a knife to remove the charred skin from the eggplants (leaving a few flecks is OK) and slice the flesh into thick strips. Transfer to a bowl.

Give the tofu a good squeeze to remove some of the liquid and crumble it over the eggplant. Combine the chilli paste, soy sauce, garlic, maple syrup and Chinese five-spice in a small bowl, then pour this over the eggplant and tofu and mix well. Set aside to marinate until required.

Meanwhile, punch down the risen dough and knead for 2 minutes to remove any air bubbles. Use a rolling pin and a bit of elbow grease to roll out the dough until it's about ½ cm (¼ in) thick. If you keep turning the dough as you roll it, you shouldn't need any extra flour, but do add a sprinkle underneath if it starts to stick.

Use a pastry brush to spread a small amount of the canola oil over the surface of the dough. Use a glass or cup to press out rounds of dough, twisting the rim to cut out each piece. Fold the rounds in half so that the oiled side is on the inside, then sit the dough rounds on cut-out squares of baking paper just larger than the dough rounds.

Bunch up any extra dough, then roll it out again and follow the same process to make a few extra bao. Place the prepared bao on a tray, then use your rolling pin to gently roll the folded bao to create a smooth surface. Cover with a tea towel and set aside for 30 minutes or until risen.

Prepare a large steamer.

Steam the bao in groups of six for 12 minutes. While they are steaming, heat the remaining canola oil in a frying pan over medium heat. Add the marinated eggplant and tofu mixture and cook, stirring frequently and scraping up any bits that stick to the base of the pan, for 5 minutes or until heated through.

Open up the bao and remove the baking paper. Smear ½ teaspoon of chilli paste inside each bao, then stuff in 2 teaspoons of the prepared filling followed by a little of the pickled veg, coriander and fried shallots.

Souvlaki

Ingredients

juice of 2 lemons
4 teaspoons chopped oregano leaves
2 teaspoons garlic powder
1 teaspoon sweet paprika
1 teaspoon sea salt
1 teaspoon freshly ground black pepper
500 g (1 lb 2 oz) Seitan chickpea chicken
  (see page 163 or use store-bought), cut
  into bite-sized chunks
olive oil, for drizzling, if needed
4 Lebanese flatbreads
115 g (4 oz) Tzatziki mayonnaise
  (see page 166)
fries, to serve

Greek salad

1 Lebanese (short) cucumber, halved
  lengthways and sliced
250 g (9 oz) cherry tomatoes, halved
1 red onion, thinly sliced
80 g (2¾ oz/½ cup) pitted Kalamata
  olives, halved
½ green capsicum (bell pepper),
  thinly sliced
sea salt and freshly ground black pepper
olive oil, for drizzling
pinch of dried oregano
100 g (3½ oz) dairy-free feta, broken
  into chunks (optional)

Every component of this recipe is delicious on its own: marinated skewered seitan, hot chips dipped in tzatziki mayonnaise and fresh Greek salad with tangy blobs of feta. But when you wrap these elements together in warm flatbread, you create the most blessed of Greek flavour combinations that Zeus himself would descend Mount Olympus for.

To make the Greek salad, combine the cucumber, tomato, onion, olives and capsicum in a large bowl. Season well with salt and pepper, drizzle over a little olive oil and add the dried oregano. Toss through the feta (if using) and set aside.

Combine the lemon juice, fresh oregano, garlic powder, paprika, salt and pepper in a shallow bowl. Add the seitan chickpea chicken and toss well to coat in the marinade. Divide the seitan chickpea chicken into four portions and place onto bamboo skewers.

Preheat a chargrill pan over high heat. Add the skewers, drizzling any extra marinade over the top. If needed, drizzle a little olive oil over the top and place a heavy pan over the skewers to press irregular pieces of the skewered 'meat' onto the hot pan. Cook, rotating frequently, until heated through and char marks appear on all sides of the 'meat'. Remove the skewers from the pan and set aside.

Add the flatbreads to the hot pan one at a time, flipping until warmed through. Transfer to plates.

Slide the 'meat' off the skewers onto the flatbreads. Divide the Greek salad and tzatziki mayonnaise among the flatbreads and serve with the fries on the side or, better yet, inside.

Falafel and tabbouleh wraps

Ingredients

10 Lebanese flatbreads
olive oil, for brushing
1 x quantity cooked Falafel (see page 162)

Quinoa tabbouleh

200 g (7 oz/1 cup) white quinoa
½ bunch spring onions (scallions),
    finely chopped
3 bunches flat-leaf parsley, leaves picked
    and finely chopped
2 bunches mint, leaves picked and
    finely chopped
6 tomatoes, finely chopped
½ teaspoon ground allspice
1 teaspoon sea salt
80 ml (2½ fl oz/⅓ cup) freshly squeezed
    lemon juice

To serve

hummus
tahini
pickled cabbage
hot sauce
fried cauliflower
pickles
lemon juice

Falafel wraps were once the only vegan fast-food option around, but those days are thankfully gone and we can now enjoy them instead of begrudgingly eating them for the umpteenth time this week. You can make these wraps in advance but you won't want to when you try freshly cooked falafel, snugly wrapped in warm bread overflowing with extra fillings. Choose from hummus, tahini, pickled cabbage, hot sauce, fried cauliflower, pickles and lemon juice to add to your wrap before serving.

To make the quinoa tabbouleh, thoroughly rinse the quinoa to remove its bitterness, then place in a small saucepan over medium heat and toast, stirring, for 2 minutes. Add 500 ml (17 fl oz/2 cups) water and bring to the boil. Reduce the heat to a simmer and cook for 15–20 minutes, until most of the water is absorbed and the quinoa is cooked through. Remove from the heat and fluff the quinoa with a fork. Set aside to cool in a large bowl.

Add the spring onion, herbs, tomato, allspice and salt to the cooled quinoa and mix to combine. Pour over the lemon juice and mix again.

Heat a large frying pan over medium heat. Lightly brush the flatbreads with olive oil and warm them, one at a time in the pan, for about 30 seconds on each side.

Divide the quinoa tabbouleh and falafel among the wraps. Top with your choice of additional fillings, roll up and serve immediately.

Satay tofu banh mi

Ingredients

4 Vietnamese rolls or long crusty rolls
Mayonnaise (see page 165 or use
    store-bought vegan mayonnaise), for
    spreading (optional)
2 bunches coriander (cilantro), sprigs
    separated, plus a few leaves to garnish
1 long cucumber, sliced into batons
2 bird's eye chillies, thinly sliced
crushed peanuts, to serve
fried shallots, to serve (optional)

Pickled veg

1 carrot, cut into long thin batons
⅓ daikon (white radish), cut into long
    thin batons
½ fresh jalapeno chilli, roughly chopped
185 ml (6½ fl oz/¾ cup) rice wine vinegar
    or white vinegar (or use a mix of both)
2 tablespoons granulated sugar
1 teaspoon sea salt

Caramelised tofu

500 g (1 lb 2 oz) firm tofu
110 g (4 oz/½ cup) granulated sugar
80 ml (2½ fl oz/⅓ cup) vegan fish sauce
    (or substitute dark soy sauce)
1 large red onion, thinly sliced
½ teaspoon freshly ground black pepper
½ teaspoon all-purpose curry powder
1 tablespoon white vinegar or freshly
    squeezed lime juice
2 tablespoons smooth peanut butter, plus
    extra for spreading (optional)

Tangy, spicy, sweet, savoury, fresh and crunchy, this sandwich is perfect for those who want a little bit of everything. The tofu is cooked in a savoury caramel just to make sure every part of your palate gets a hit. Use your hands to press the soft bread into the crust so you can cram in an unrealistic quantity of fillings.

To make the pickled veg, place the carrot, daikon and jalapeno in a clean jar. Place 125 ml (4 fl oz/½ cup) water in a saucepan, along with the vinegar, sugar and salt and bring to the boil. Once the sugar has dissolved, pour the vinegar mixture into the jar. Set aside for 1 hour to pickle.

To make the caramelised tofu, wrap the tofu in paper towel and place under a heavy object for 20 minutes. Chop the tofu into 2 cm (¾ in) cubes.

Place the sugar in a frying pan over medium heat and cook, shaking and agitating the pan occasionally, for 5 minutes or until beginning to turn to liquid. Pour in the fish sauce and stir to combine. Add the red onion and let the mixture bubble for 5 minutes. Stir through the pepper, then toss in the tofu cubes. Reduce the heat to low and cook, stirring occasionally, for 15 minutes. Towards the end of the cooking time, stir in the curry powder and vinegar or lime juice. Remove a few spoonfuls of sauce and reserve for drizzling over your finished banh mi.

Stir the peanut butter into the pan, then remove from the heat and cover to keep warm until required. Use a bread knife to cut the rolls almost in half, leaving them still attached on one side. Use your hands to press in some of the soft bread to make room for more filling. If you like, smear on some mayonnaise or peanut butter before proceeding.

Stuff each roll with the caramelised tofu and pickled veg, coriander sprigs and cucumber batons. Scatter over the chilli, crushed peanuts and fried shallots (if using) and finish with a few coriander leaves to complete the job.

You can also use store-bought vegan burger patties if you're in a rush.

The Big Zac

Ingredients

20 g (¾ oz) dried shiitake mushrooms

400 g (14 oz) tin black beans, rinsed and drained, reserving 60 ml (2 fl oz/¼ cup) aquafaba

90 g (3 oz/¾ cup) small chunk TVP (Textured Vegetable Protein)

3 tablespoons tomato ketchup

3 tablespoons barbecue sauce

1 tablespoon liquid smoke

135 g (5 oz) gluten flour, plus 2 tablespoons extra if needed

1 tablespoon beef-style stock powder

2 teaspoons onion powder

½ teaspoon freshly ground black pepper

120 ml (4 fl oz) olive oil

8 slices dairy-free American-style cheese

8 sesame-covered burger buns

2 large handfuls shredded iceberg lettuce

½ white onion, finely chopped

2 sweet and spicy dill pickles (gherkins), sliced into rounds

Big Zac secret sauce

135 g (5 oz/½ cup) Mayonnaise (see page 165 or use store-bought vegan mayonnaise)

2 tablespoons gherkin relish

2 teaspoons Dijon or American mustard

1 teaspoon white vinegar

½ teaspoon granulated sugar

up to ½ teaspoon smoked paprika

¼ teaspoon onion powder

¼ teaspoon garlic powder

An iconic flavour combination, which I have veganised and bears absolutely no resemblance to a burger with a similar name. It's all handily wrapped up in a bun so you can eat it on the go while avoiding a cease and desist from a multinational fast-food corporation.

Preheat the oven to 180°C (350°F).

To make the Big Zac secret sauce, combine the ingredients in a bowl and set aside. Place the dried shiitake mushrooms in a food processor and blitz to a powder. Add the black beans and process until smooth.

In a large bowl, combine the TVP, reserved aquafaba, ketchup, barbecue sauce and liquid smoke. Mix in the black bean mixture and set aside. In another large bowl, combine the gluten flour, stock powder, onion powder and pepper. Stir the prepared TVP mixture into the dry ingredients until the mixture comes together. Knead until everything is fully combined, adding the extra gluten flour if needed to bring it together into a ball. Divide into quarters and press each quarter into two patties.

Line a baking tray with baking paper and place the patties on top. Sprinkle over 125 ml (4 fl oz/½ cup) water. Cover the patties with another sheet of baking paper and bake for 1 hour, flipping at the halfway mark and sprinkling over another ½ cup water. Check every so often to ensure that the patties aren't browning up too much – they should be mostly dry by the time the hour is up. Remove from the oven and set aside to cool.

Heat half the oil in a frying pan over medium heat. Add four of the patties and press with a spatula to flatten them slightly. Cook for 5 minutes, then flip and cook the other sides for 5 minutes. Flip again and place two cheese slices on top of each patty. Continue to cook until the cheese starts to melt, then remove from the pan. Heat the remaining oil and cook the remaining patties.

While the patties are cooking, use a bread knife to halve the buns. Four of the top halves won't be required, so set these away for later use. Lightly toast the buns.

Spread a generous amount of Big Zac secret sauce over the bottom half of four burger buns. Scatter lettuce over the sauce and top with a cheesy burger patty, cheese side down. Add a little onion and place the remaining bottom bun halves on top.

Continue to build the burgers with another round of sauce and lettuce and then top with the pickle and remaining patties. Scatter over the remaining onion and finish with the bun tops.

Double 'beef' and 'bacon' burgers

Ingredients

120 ml (4 fl oz) olive oil

8 unfried Big Zac burger patties
   (see page 77)

16 slices dairy-free American-style cheese

4 burger buns

4 sheets chewy Rice paper bacon, cut into
   strips (see page 164)

½ white onion, finely chopped OR 8 Onion
   rings (see page 22)

tomato ketchup, to serve

your favourite mustard, to serve

This burger comes with double the lack of beef AND twice the no bacon. It does come loaded, however, with two vegan versions of each component plus a few onion rings wedged in for good measure. I'm sure nobody will have any complaints, at least because it's rude to speak with your mouth full and this bad boy is one hell of a mouthful.

Heat half the olive oil in a frying pan over medium heat. Add four of the patties and press with a spatula to flatten them slightly. Cook for 5 minutes, then flip and cook the other side for 5 minutes. Flip again and place two cheese slices on top of each patty. Continue to cook until the cheese starts to melt, then remove from the pan and repeat with the remaining oil, patties and cheese.

While the patties are cooking, use a bread knife to halve the buns and lightly toast the cut sides.

Place a cooked patty on the bottom half of each of the burger buns, cheese side up. Top with the remaining cheesy patties and add one or two strips of rice paper bacon. Sprinkle the onion or rest two onion rings on top and squirt over some ketchup. Spread mustard on the remaining burger bun halves, close up the burgers and you're good to go.

You can also use store-bought vegan burger patties if you're in a rush.

Bhaji burgers

Ingredients

canola oil, for deep-frying
2 long green chillies, finely chopped
juice of 1 lime
90 g (3 oz) Mayonnaise (see page 165 or use store-bought vegan mayonnaise)
100 g (3½ oz) white cabbage, shredded
80 g (2¾ oz) red cabbage, shredded
½ carrot, grated
4 fancy seeded burger buns
150 g (5½ oz) mango chutney

Bhajis

2 onions, thinly sliced and core removed
6 curry leaves, finely chopped
1 bunch coriander (cilantro), leaves picked and finely chopped
1½ teaspoons nigella seeds
¾ teaspoon sea salt
¾ teaspoon ground cumin
½ teaspoon ground turmeric
½ teaspoon chilli powder
55 g (2 oz/½ cup) chickpea flour (besan)
35 g (1¼ oz) rice flour
60 ml (2 fl oz/¼ cup) freshly squeezed lemon juice
1 tablespoon olive oil

This combination of spiced onion bhaji, chilli and lime slaw and mango chutney is tantalising just as long as nobody points out it sort of looks like a spider trying to crawl out of the burger. Quick, eat it before it escapes!

To make the bhajis, combine the onion, curry leaves, half the coriander, the nigella seeds, salt, cumin, turmeric and chilli powder in a large bowl. Add the chickpea and rice flours and mix well. Pour the lemon juice, olive oil and 3 tablespoons water over the mixture and stir thoroughly until a thin batter clings to the onion.

Heat the canola oil in a large heavy-based saucepan over high heat. Test if the oil is ready by inserting a wooden skewer or the handle of a wooden spoon into the oil; if it begins to bubble quickly then you're ready to go.

Divide the bhaji mixture into eight portions and group loosely together in the bowl, creating clumps while also leaving small gaps between the onion strands. Use a spatula to lower the bhajis into the oil and fry for 2–3 minutes, until golden brown, flipping regularly to ensure they cook evenly. Transfer to a plate lined with paper towel to drain.

Meanwhile, combine the chilli, lime juice and mayonnaise in one bowl and the cabbages and carrot in another bowl. Stir the mayonnaise mixture through the slaw mix, along with the remaining coriander.

Slice the buns in half and spread the mango chutney on the top half of each bun. Spoon the slaw onto the other side. Rest two bhajis on top of the slaw and top with the chutney-covered bun halves. Press down firmly so the sauces glue everything together.

Bratwursts

Ingredients

100 ml (3½ fl oz) olive oil
1 large brown onion, finely chopped
125 g (4½ oz) mushrooms, finely chopped
8 garlic cloves, finely chopped
250 ml (8½ fl oz/1 cup) Guinness or
    dark beer
1 tablespoon soy sauce
1 tablespoon Vegemite
2 teaspoons liquid smoke
270 g (9½ oz) gluten flour, plus extra
    if needed
20 g (¾ oz) nutritional yeast
3 beef-style stock cubes, crumbled
1 tablespoon granulated sugar
1½ teaspoons dried marjoram
½ teaspoon freshly ground black pepper
1 teaspoon ground ginger
1 teaspoon smoked paprika
½ teaspoon chilli powder
½ teaspoon ground nutmeg

To serve

6 hot-dog rolls
sauerkraut
tomato ketchup
American mustard
potato chips (crisps)

Snags for every occasion: from a simple hot dog with a squeeze of sauce to dressed up with sides galore. This recipe calls for 250 ml (8½ fl oz/1 cup) of Guinness which is less than a bottle holds, so pick this dish for dinner if you need an excuse to crack open a beer. Otherwise, pour the rest of the beer over the brats as they fry and apologise to the designated driver.

Heat 1 tablespoon of the olive oil in a small frying pan over high heat. Sauté the onion for 5 minutes, then add the mushroom and sauté for a further 5 minutes. Add the garlic and cook, stirring occasionally, until the mixture starts to catch on the base of the pan.

Combine the beer, soy sauce, Vegemite and liquid smoke in a bowl. Pour this mixture into the mushroom mixture and use it to deglaze the pan. Remove from the heat and purée until smooth using a stick blender.

Fill a saucepan with water, set a steamer over the top and place over high heat until boiling. Reduce the heat to a simmer and cover.

Combine the remaining ingredients in a large bowl. Add the blended mushroom mixture and stir to incorporate. Knead with your hands for about 1 minute, adding a little more gluten flour if needed to bring the mixture together. It's ready when it's softly sticky and springy and able to be picked up.

Divide the dough into six portions. Place each portion in a square of biodegradable plastic wrap, then roll into sausages inside the plastic wrap, twisting the ends to secure. Don't wrap them too tightly as they will expand while steaming. Once wrapped, use your hands to gently massage the sausages within the wrap to round and smooth them out. Place in the steamer for 40 minutes.

Remove the sausages from the steamer and allow to cool before unwrapping them.

Heat the remaining oil in a frying pan over medium–high heat. Add the sausages and cook for about 8 minutes, moving them around constantly for the first few minutes so they don't catch on the base of the pan. By the end of cooking, the sausages should be soft but cooked through with a firm exterior that's starting to char.

Stuff the hot-dog rolls with sauerkraut and place a sausage on top. Squirt over ketchup and mustard and serve with potato chips.

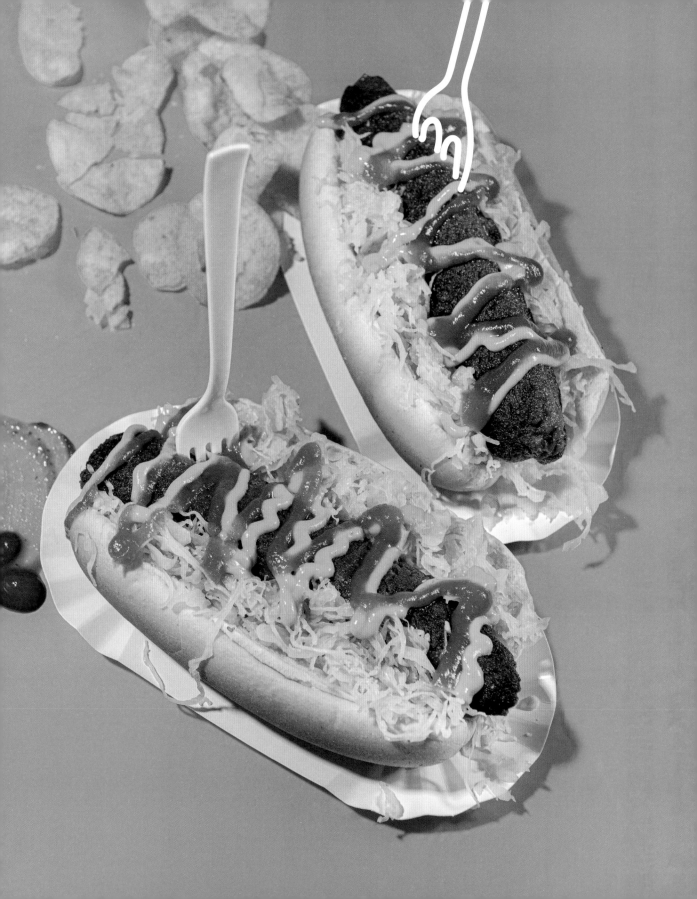

The kogo

Ingredients

800 g frozen crinkle-cut fries
6 vegan hot dogs
plain (all-purpose) flour, for dusting
canola oil, for deep-frying
sea salt
hot sauce and/or tomato ketchup, to serve

Batter

150 g (5½ oz/1 cup) plain (all-purpose) flour
2 tablespoons aquafaba
2 tablespoons granulated sugar
2 teaspoons baking powder
1 teaspoon sea salt
250 ml (8½ fl oz/1 cup) soy milk

Honey–mustard sauce

65 g (2¼ oz/¼ cup) Mayonnaise (see
    page 165 or use store-bought vegan
    mayonnaise)
2½ tablespoons Dijon or American
    mustard
1½ tablespoons Vegan honey (see
    page 170) or rice malt syrup
dash of vinegar, sea salt and chilli powder,
    to taste

Forget what you've heard, South Korea is the new home of the hot dog. In case the photo doesn't do it justice, let's walk through what goes into this feast precariously loaded onto a stick known as a kogo. It's a corn dog crusted with crinkle-cut fries and zig-zagged with homemade honey–mustard sauce and ketchup. Yep, you read that correctly. If you don't have chips to hand, you can substitute them for panko breadcrumbs at a pinch.

Defrost the chips to fridge temperature. Sit the hot dogs on a work surface until they come to room temperature. Slide the hot dogs onto bamboo skewers and dust them in flour.

Cut the chips into 2 cm (¾ in) long chunks and place in a shallow bowl.

Heat the canola oil in a large heavy-based saucepan over medium–high heat. Test if the oil is ready by inserting a wooden skewer or the handle of a wooden spoon into the oil; if it begins to bubble quickly then you're ready to go.

Mix the batter ingredients except the soy milk in a tall glass. Slowly whisk in the milk, stopping when you reach a thick batter. Dip each skewered dog into the batter and swirl to completely coat. Transfer to the bowl with the chips and use your hands to press the chips into the batter (you'll be surprised at how many you can get on there). Transfer the dogs to a large slotted spoon and press any remaining chips into the dogs, drizzling extra batter on top if needed.

Using the skewers as handles, immediately place the hot dogs into the hot oil. If needed, trim the skewers first to fit or just leave the sticks sitting out of the pan and use them to turn the dogs. Fry the hot dogs for 5–6 minutes, until golden on all sides. Test to make sure the batter is cooked through and the hot dog is hot. If not, return to the oil for a few more minutes.

While the hot dogs are frying, combine the honey–mustard sauce ingredients in a bowl.

Place the hot dogs on a plate lined with paper towel to drain and season with salt. Cover in a tablespoon of honey–mustard sauce and squeeze over hot sauce and/or ketchup.

Currywurst

Ingredients

2 tablespoons olive oil
1 small onion, finely chopped
2 tablespoons all-purpose curry powder
1 teaspoon chilli powder
2 tablespoons tomato paste
   (concentrated purée)
400 g (14 oz) tin cherry tomatoes
3 tablespoons vegan Worcestershire sauce
2 tablespoons white vinegar
1 tablespoon granulated sugar
sea salt and freshly ground black pepper
6 Bratwurst sausages (see page 82)
splash of your favourite beer (optional)

Fry up those leftover bratwursts and put together this easy curried ketchup to throw over the top. An extra pinch of curry powder, along with mustard, sauerkraut, crinkle-cut chips (fries), mashed potato or potato in any form are welcome additions to the plate to complete a hearty meal.

Heat half the olive oil in a frying pan over medium heat. Add the onion and cook, stirring frequently, for 10 minutes or until just starting to brown. Stir in the curry powder and chilli powder until fragrant, then add the tomato paste and stir again.

Add the tomatoes, Worcestershire sauce, vinegar and sugar, season with salt and pepper and bring to the boil. Reduce the heat to low and simmer for 20 minutes, pressing down on the tomatoes to release their juices. Remove from the heat and allow to cool slightly. Use a stick blender to combine the mixture into a smooth curried ketchup, adding a splash of water if the mixture is very thick.

Splash the remaining oil into another frying pan over high heat. Add the sausages and cook, turning frequently, for about 8 minutes, until browned and cooked through. Add a splash of beer every now and then if you need an excuse to crack one open. When done, use tongs to transfer the bratwurst to a plate, then cut into thick slices and smother in the hot curried ketchup. The choice of sides is endless but should probably include potato in some form.

UPSIZE

Coming up are big feasts made for sharing: the potluck jackpot. These recipes are perfect for not only bringing people together, but kick-starting a fling with ingredients you might not have had time to get to know yet. Break up with seitan and try novel ways of making meat alternatives using jackfruit, or try your hand at making banana blossom–battered 'fish', TVP Tex-Mex tacos or loaded baked potatoes with rice paper bacon. Of course, you'll want to rekindle your relationship with seitan at some point to make Korean fried 'chicken' or the meat loather's pizza.

This chapter is also home to my signature recipe – Southern-fried 'chicken' drumsticks – a global hit with an edible bone made out of cauliflower clad in chicken-like jackfruit flesh and coated in spices. This is the original vegan chicken drumstick that you can make at home. The others are all imitations. Then again, so are my drumsticks.

Nachos

Ingredients

420 g (15 oz) tin black beans, rinsed
and drained
2 teaspoons minced garlic
sea salt
½ teaspoon ground cumin
juice of 1 lime
1 x quantity Taco mince (see page 112)
1 teaspoon Taco seasoning (see page 112),
plus extra if needed
2 tablespoons olive oil
2 teaspoons Tajin
200 g (7 oz) bag tortilla chips
150 g (5½ oz/½ cup) Salsa (see page 38)
125 g (4½ oz/½ cup) Cashew queso dip
without salsa (see page 38)
210 g (7½ oz) tinned sweetcorn kernels,
rinsed and drained
40 g (1½ oz/⅓) cup shredded
dairy-free cheese
3 tablespoons minced pickled jalapenos
1 avocado, diced
125 g (4½ oz) Sour cream (see page 169)
coriander (cilantro) leaves, to serve
(optional)

These nachos include all of the toppings you can dream of, but if you want to keep things simple, just pick a few and nobody will be any the wiser. Just make sure you use tortilla chips, vegan mince or beans and some salsa as your base.

Preheat the oven to 160°C (320°F). Line a baking tray with baking paper.

Place the beans, garlic and a big pinch of salt in a saucepan over medium–high heat. Cook, stirring occasionally, for 8 minutes, then stir through the ground cumin. Cook for a further 2 minutes, then remove from the heat and stir through the lime juice and 60 ml (2 fl oz/¼ cup) water. Transfer the bean mixture to a food processor and blitz until smooth, adding a little more water if the mixture is very dry.

Place the taco mince and taco seasoning in a dry frying pan over high heat. Cook until the spices become aromatic, then add the olive oil and sauté the mince until crisp. Remove from the heat and taste, adding more taco seasoning if desired.

Sprinkle the Tajin into the bag of tortilla chips and shake to distribute the spice mix. Spread half the tortilla chips over the baking tray. Using a teaspoon, blob half the puréed beans, salsa, cashew queso dip, sweetcorn, shredded cheese and jalapeno over the tortilla chips. Scatter half the fried mince over the top and bake for 10 minutes.

Remove the nachos from the oven and repeat the layering with the same ingredients, except this time scatter the shredded cheese and corn on top. Return to the oven for a further 5 minutes. (If your cheese isn't melting, use the back of a spoon to press down on the cheese to help it out.)

Preheat the grill (broiler) to high and grill the nachos, keeping a close eye on them to ensure they don't burn, and grill for about 5 minutes, until the cheese is completely melted and golden.

Remove the nachos from the grill and spoon the avocado and sour cream over the top. Garnish with coriander leaves or don't. It's time to tuck in.

Southern-fried 'chicken' drumsticks

Ingredients

2 × 565 g (1 lb 4 oz) tins young green
  jackfruit, rinsed and drained
375 ml (12½ fl oz/1½ cups) chicken-
  style stock
2 teaspoons nutritional yeast
1 teaspoon onion powder
10 drops liquid smoke
1 cauliflower
185 ml (6½ fl oz/¾ cup) aquafaba
canola oil, for deep-frying

Drumstick spice mix

110 g (4 oz/¾ cup) plain (all-purpose) flour,
  plus extra for dusting
1 tablespoon brown sugar
½ teaspoon sea salt
½ teaspoon smoked paprika
½ teaspoon onion powder
½ teaspoon chilli powder
¼ teaspoon garlic powder
¼ teaspoon celery salt
¼ teaspoon ground sage
¼ teaspoon ground allspice
¼ teaspoon dried basil
pinch of dried oregano
½ teaspoon kala namak (Indian black salt
  or use extra sea salt)
1 teaspoon MSG/torula yeast (optional)

Jackfruit is often mistakenly labelled as 'vegan pulled pork' by those who have merely drowned it in barbecue sauce. Instead, try this recipe which allows the jackfruit's stringy texture and ability to absorb flavour sing. Track down a tin at your local Asian supermarket; you're looking for the young green jackfruit in brine, as the ripened versions are sweetened in syrup and only appropriate for desserts. The jackfruit is actually a cousin to durian, so don't bother messing with the fresh stuff unless you absolutely have to.

Cut away the hard core from the jackfruit, then squeeze each piece so that any seeds pop out and any excess liquid is removed. Gently pull the jackfruit pieces to make them stringy, then rinse away the remaining brine under warm running water. Squeeze the jackfruit dry.

Place the jackfruit in a saucepan with the stock, nutritional yeast, onion powder and liquid smoke. Bring the mixture to the boil, stirring frequently, for 10 minutes, then reduce the heat to low and cook for a further 10 minutes or until the liquid has evaporated. Remove from the heat and set aside to cool. Divide the mixture into four portions.

Starting at the base, cut the cauliflower into quarters. You want to keep the stalk attached to the florets as this will be your 'chicken bone'. Use a small knife to carefully remove the leaves. Trim the stalks into a rounded bone shape, then cut off the majority of the florets so you are left with a basic chicken drumstick shape. Use the florets to make the Southern fried cauliflower on page 34.

Place a large square of plastic wrap on your work surface and spoon half of one portion of the jackfruit mixture towards the edge closest to you. Lay a cauliflower drumstick on top of the jackfruit mixture with the stalk sticking out the end of the plastic wrap. Add the remaining half portion of jackfruit mixture on top, filling in and loosely covering the florets.

Pick up the four corners of the plastic wrap and fold them over the jackfruit mixture, twisting to enclose the jackfruit around the florets. Once sealed, gently squeeze the jackfruit mixture to let the excess liquid run down the 'bone'. Use your hands to mould the jackfruit inside the wrap to evenly cover the cauliflower and

mush it into the perfect shape. Repeat for each cauliflower 'bone', then place the drumsticks on a tray in your freezer for at least 1 hour to firm up.

Combine the spice mix ingredients in a large bowl and pour the aquafaba into a separate shallow bowl.

Heat the canola oil in a large heavy-based saucepan over medium–high heat. Test if the oil is ready by inserting a wooden skewer or the handle of a wooden spoon into the oil; if it begins to bubble quickly then you're ready to go.

Once the drumsticks have firmed up, take them out of the freezer and unwrap the plastic wrap – this is where it gets tricky, because as soon as the jackfruit hits the aquafaba it will want to fall apart, so you need to work quickly.

Holding a drumstick in one hand, drizzle over enough aquafaba to coat, then place the drumstick into the spice mix and toss extra on top to coat. Use floured hands to press the drumstick back into shape if necessary, then repeat the coating process and set aside while you repeat with the remaining drumsticks.

Cook the drumsticks in two batches, turning constantly, for 3–5 minutes, until golden on all sides. (Use tongs to turn the drumsticks and make sure you grip them by the fleshy part so they maintain their shape.) Drain on paper towels and serve immediately, picking your jaw up off the ground once you realise how good they are!

'Fish' and chips

Ingredients

2 × 510 g (1 lb 2 oz) tins banana blossoms
   in brine, drained
canola oil, for deep-frying
1 x quantity cooked frozen fries
   (see page 45)
Tartar sauce (see page 168), to serve
lemon wedges, to serve

Marinade

2 spring onions (scallions), finely chopped
1–2 nori sheets, finely chopped
2 cm (¾ in) knob of ginger, minced
2 garlic cloves, minced
80 ml (2½ fl oz/⅓ cup) vegan white wine

Batter

150 g (5½ oz/1 cup) self-raising flour
sea salt and freshly ground black pepper
250 ml (8½ fl oz/1 cup) beer or soda water

If you're uncomfortable with this dish looking realistic, serve it as a fried mermaid for an unrealistic twist instead. Seaweed, white wine and ginger lend 'fishy' flavours, but for something that tastes just like it came from the ocean you'll need to add plastic or a pinch of microbeads.

Rinse the banana blossom under running water, squeezing out as much brine as possible, then place in a bowl.

Combine the marinade ingredients in a separate bowl, then add to the banana blossom and massage through, separating the pieces as you go. Cover the banana blossom with cold water, then cover in plastic wrap and marinate for 2–24 hours in the fridge, tossing occasionally.

To prepare the batter, season the flour with salt and pepper, then place it in the freezer with the beer or soda water to get super cold ahead of frying.

Remove the marinated banana blossom from the fridge, scoop out one-quarter and squeeze together. The goal is to wring out the majority of the liquid, but keep just a little moistness and flavour. This action should also bring the blossoms together into a 'fillet'. Coat in a little of your cold seasoned flour to create a dry exterior. Repeat with the remaining banana blossom to make four 'fillets'.

Heat the canola oil in a large heavy-based saucepan over medium–high heat. Test if the oil is ready by inserting a wooden skewer or the handle of a wooden spoon into the oil; if it begins to bubble quickly then you're ready to go.

Now it's time to prepare your batter. Slowly pour the cold beer or soda into the flour, stopping intermittently to fully incorporate the liquid before adding more until the batter just comes together. Use immediately while cold and the beer or water is still bubbly.

Dip each 'fillet' into the batter, scooping the batter around it. Slide two battered 'fillets' into the oil in a fluid motion and cook for 2–4 minutes, until golden and crisp. Drain on a plate lined with paper towel and repeat with the remaining 'fillets'.

Serve your banana blossom 'fish' with freshly fried chips, tartar sauce and lemon wedges.

Cheesy eggplant parmigiana

Ingredients

sea salt
3 eggplants (aubergines), peeled and cut
   lengthways into ½ cm (¼ in) thick slices
cooking oil spray
210 g (7½ oz) shredded dairy-free cheese
chopped basil leaves, to serve

Tomato sauce

15 ripe tomatoes
1 tablespoon olive oil
3 onions, finely chopped
10 garlic cloves, finely chopped
95 g (3¼ oz) tomato paste (concentrated
   purée)
1½ teaspoons dried basil
1½ tablespoons dried oregano
1 tablespoon granulated sugar

Italian crumb

185 ml (6½ fl oz/¾ cup) aquafaba
75 g (2¾ oz/½ cup) plain (all-purpose) flour
120 g (4½ oz/2 cups) panko breadcrumbs
30 g (1 oz/½ cup) nutritional yeast
2 teaspoons sea salt
2 teaspoons dried basil
1 teaspoon freshly ground black pepper

The most delicious versions of this dish are born from hours of slowly simmering the sauce and cooking the eggplant until golden. Cooking with love is optional as you can easily substitute cooking with hatred, due to the length of time this recipe takes; just make sure you're cooking with passion.

To make the tomato sauce, place the tomatoes in a food processor and blend to a purée.

Heat the olive oil in a frying pan over medium heat. Add the onion and sauté for 10–15 minutes, until translucent. Add the garlic and sauté for 2–3 minutes, then add the tomato paste and dried herbs and stir through. Add the puréed tomatoes and sugar, then bring to a simmer and cook, stirring occasionally, for at least 1 hour – pay attention to the raw smell of the tomatoes, this will be replaced with a rich scent, telling you the sauce is ready. You can get on with the rest of the recipe while this bubbles away.

Liberally salt the surface of the eggplant, then wrap in paper towel and place a heavy object on top for 20 minutes to release their moisture. Unwrap the eggplant, wipe away the salt and moisture and set aside.

Preheat the oven to 220°C (430°F) and line two baking trays with baking paper.

To make the Italian crumb, place the aquafaba and flour in separate shallow bowls. In a third shallow bowl, combine the breadcrumbs, half the nutritional yeast, the salt, basil and pepper.

Working with one slice at a time, dip the eggplant into the aquafaba before coating in the flour. Dip back into the aquafaba and then coat in the breadcrumb mixture, using your hands to firmly press the breadcrumbs into the eggplant until they hold, creating a consistent coating. Set aside on the prepared trays. Spray the eggplant on both sides with cooking oil spray, then bake in the oven for 30 minutes or until crispy and golden. If you've got the time, you may instead like to pan-fry these until golden on both sides to add extra calories (flavour).

Reduce the oven temperature to 180°C (350°F).

Generously spread one quarter of the tomato sauce over the base of a large baking dish. Sprinkle two teaspoons of the remaining nutritional yeast over the top and cover with a layer of baked eggplant and a good scattering of shredded cheese. Repeat this layering, finishing with a final layer of tomato sauce, shredded cheese and any left-over breadcrumb mixture. Bake in the oven for 20 minutes, or until heated through and the cheese has melted.

Scatter a few chopped basil leaves over the top and serve.

Butternut pumpkin mac 'n' cheese

Serves 3–4

Ingredients

200–300 g (7–10½ oz) butternut pumpkin (squash), peeled, deseeded and roughly chopped
200 g (7 oz) dried macaroni
1 tablespoon olive oil
1½ tablespoons plain (all-purpose) flour
310 ml (10½ fl oz/1¼ cups) soy milk
125 g (4½ oz/1 cup) shredded dairy-free cheese
1 teaspoon garlic powder
1 teaspoon Dijon mustard
2 tablespoons nutritional yeast
½ freshly grated nutmeg or ⅛ teaspoon ground nutmeg
1 teaspoon finely chopped thyme leaves
⅛ teaspoon chilli powder
½ teaspoon ground sage
sea salt and freshly ground black pepper
30 g (1 oz/½ cup) panko breadcrumbs

Hidden veggies are a dead trend, joining other failed food fads, such as salads suspended in jell-o, in the hall of shame. It's time to proudly display your love of vegetables, with lumps of pumpkin stirred through this mac 'n' cheese instead of being snuck into the cheese sauce.

Preheat the oven to 200°C (400°F). Line a baking tray with baking paper.

Place the pumpkin on the prepared tray and bake for 20 minutes or until soft and cooked through. Transfer the pumpkin to a bowl and lazily mash it with a fork to create a lumpy mash. Reduce the oven temperature to 160°C (320°F).

Cook the macaroni according to the packet instructions until just before al dente. Drain and set aside in a medium baking dish.

Heat the olive oil in a saucepan over medium heat. Sift in the flour and stir constantly for 2 minutes until you have a roux. Once the roux starts to bubble, gradually whisk in the soy milk a little at a time. When all the milk has been incorporated, stir in three-quarters of the cheese, the garlic powder, mustard and nutritional yeast and cook, stirring, for 8–10 minutes, until thickened. Remove from the heat and stir through the nutmeg, thyme, chilli and sage.

Pour the cheese sauce over the cooked pasta, add the mashed pumpkin and gently mix to combine. Season with salt and pepper, then scatter the remaining cheese and the breadcrumbs over the top.

Transfer to the oven and bake for 30 minutes or until the breadcrumbs are crisp and golden.

Allow the mac 'n' cheese to cool for 10 minutes before serving.

Spanakopita

Ingredients

500 g (1 lb 2 oz) mixed greens, such as
   spinach, kale, silverbeet (Swiss chard),
   green beans and leeks
185 ml (6½ fl oz/¾¾ cup) olive oil
1 large onion, finely chopped
3 garlic cloves, finely chopped
2 spring onions (scallions), finely chopped
zest and juice of 1 lemon
1 large bunch dill, fronds picked and
   finely chopped, plus extra fronds
   to garnish
25 g (¾ oz) chickpea flour (besan)
200 g (7 oz) dairy-free feta
   (brine or oil reserved)
sea salt and freshly ground black pepper
375 g (13 oz) refrigerated dairy-free
   filo pastry
Greek salad (see page 70), to serve

A proper bunch of dill is huge, so if your local supermarket tries to pass off a measly shrub as a whole bunch, use two or three for this recipe, as dill is our star flavour! The rest of the greens are interchangeable, fresh or frozen spinach is the standard but you can use a mix of kale, silverbeet, green beans or leeks.

If using spinach, kale or silverbeet, strip the leaves from the stems, then wilt the leaves in batches in a large saucepan over medium heat. Set aside to cool completely, then finely chop. Thinly slice the green beans and leeks, if using.

In the same pan over medium heat, add a drizzle of the olive oil and fry the onion and leek for 3 minutes. If using green beans, add them in and sauté for a further 3 minutes. Add the garlic and spring onion and cook, stirring, for 2–3 minutes, until fragrant. Stir through the lemon zest and juice and dill, then remove from the heat.

Squeeze as much liquid as you can out of the wilted greens. If you think you're done, you're not. Keep squeezing until the leaves are almost dry as any remaining liquid will turn into steam and ruin the crispness of the pastry. It'll feel like you're squeezing out all the nutrients and that's because you are.

Place the wilted leaves in a large bowl and stir through the chickpea flour and a dash of the brine or oil from the feta. You can process the mixture in a food processor for a few seconds for a smoother texture, but this isn't really necessary if everything is finely chopped. Add the onion mixture, crumble in the feta and stir to combine. Season with salt and pepper.

Preheat the oven to 225°C (435°F). Line a baking tray with baking paper.

Remove the filo pastry from its packet and either proceed quickly or cover with a scarcely damp tea towel. Use a pastry brush to cover the base of the lined baking tray with olive oil, then line the tray with three sheets of filo.

Brush a little more oil over the pastry and place two sheets of filo next to each other on top (the ends will hang over the edges of the tray). Rotate the tray 90 degrees and repeat with another two sheets of filo. Keep going until you've used eight sheets of filo in total.

Spoon the filling into the baking tray and use a spatula to spread until flat and smooth. Fold the overhanging filo sheets over the mixture, drizzling and brushing the pastry with a little more oil as you go. Place two more sheets of filo over one half of the filling, then brush with oil and tuck the ends under the filled bottom of the pastry. Repeat with two more filo sheets on the other side.

Cut the spanakopita into the portion sizes you'd like before baking. Loosely crumple the remaining filo sheets to create as much texture as possible and position the sheets on top of each portion. Brush the remaining oil over the top.

Place on the middle shelf of the oven and immediately reduce the temperature to 175°C (345°F). Bake for 1 hour or until the pastry is golden and crisp, then allow to cool for 20–30 minutes.

Garnish with a few dill fronds and serve with the Greek salad.

'Beefy' lasagne

Ingredients

500 g (1 lb 2 oz) vegan mince or 200 g
(7 oz) small chunk TVP (Textured
Vegetable Protein)
625 ml (21 fl oz/2½ cups) beef-style or
vegetable stock (optional)
80 ml (2½ fl oz/⅓ cup) olive oil, plus
extra for drizzling
3 garlic cloves, minced
2½ tablespoons dried oregano
2½ tablespoons dried basil
2 tablespoons onion powder
1 teaspoon caraway seeds
¼ teaspoon chilli powder
500 g (1 lb 2 oz) tomato paste
(concentrated purée)
700 g (1 lb 9 oz) passata (puréed tomatoes)
60 ml (2 fl oz/¼ cup) vegan red wine
1 tablespoon celery salt
1 tablespoon freshly ground black pepper
1 tablespoon granulated sugar
3 dried bay leaves
8–12 large lasagne sheets

Bechamel

3 tablespoons dairy-free butter or olive oil
35 g (1¼ oz/¼ cup) plain (all-purpose) flour
560 ml (19 fl oz/2¼ cups) soy milk, plus
extra if needed
15 g (½ oz/¼ cup) nutritional yeast
1 teaspoon Dijon mustard
125 g (4½ oz/1 cup) shredded
dairy-free cheese, plus extra for
scattering (optional)

Please enjoy this lasagne recipe that probably isn't too dissimilar from most lasagne recipes you'll find on the internet, with the exception of my life story missing from the preamble and no silly comments at the bottom. Aren't cookbooks grand?

If using TVP, soak it in the stock for 10 minutes or until most of the liquid has been absorbed. Drain, reserving any unabsorbed stock.

Heat the olive oil in a large frying pan over medium heat. Add the garlic, oregano, basil, onion powder, caraway seeds and chilli powder and cook, stirring, for 2–3 minutes, until fragrant.

Add the tomato paste, passata, wine, celery salt, pepper, sugar and bay leaves. If using TVP, pour in the unabsorbed stock and enough additional water to make up 500 ml (17 fl oz/2 cups). If using vegan mince, just add the water.

Bring to a slow boil, then add the mince or soaked TVP. Reduce the heat to a simmer and cook, stirring occasionally, for 45 minutes or until reduced and thickened. Remove from the heat and fish out and discard the bay leaves.

Preheat the oven to 180°C (350°F).

Heat the butter or olive oil in a large saucepan over medium heat. Sift in the flour and stir constantly for 1–2 minutes, until you have a roux. Once the roux starts to bubble, gradually whisk in the soy milk a little at a time. When all the liquid has been added, reduce the heat to low and let the bechamel simmer, stirring frequently, for several minutes until thickened. Stir through the nutritional yeast, mustard and cheese. If the sauce is thickening too much, add a splash more soy milk, then remove from the heat and set aside.

Drizzle a little olive oil into a 30 cm x 25 cm (12 in x 10 in) baking dish, then spread a small amount of mince mixture and bechamel so that there is a thin layer coating the entire base. Add a layer of lasagne sheets, then repeat with another layer of mince and bechamel. You can also scatter extra dairy-free cheese in between each layer if you're some sort of billionaire who can afford to do so. Repeat the layering process until you reach the top of the baking dish, finishing with a layer of bechamel.

Bake for 45 minutes or until golden and bubbling. Allow to cool slightly before serving.

Okonomiyaki

Ingredients

35 g (1¼ oz) flaxseed (linseed) meal
110 ml (4 fl oz) aquafaba or water
600 g (1 lb 5 oz) cabbage, finely shredded
1 potato, grated
4 spring onions (scallions), finely chopped,
    plus extra, sliced, to serve
40 g (1½ oz) fried shallots, plus extra
    to serve
300 g (10½ oz/2 cups) plain
    (all-purpose) flour
340 ml (11½ fl oz/1⅓ cups) vegetable stock
canola oil, for cooking
Japanese mayonnaise (see page 165),
    to serve
pickled sushi ginger, to serve
shredded nori, to serve

Okonomiyaki sauce

110 ml (4 fl oz) tomato ketchup
75 ml (2½ fl oz) vegan Worcestershire
    sauce
2 tablespoons rice wine vinegar

Okonomiyaki is described by some as a Japanese cabbage pancake, and as a Japanese pizza by others with a looser grasp on the concepts of okonomiyaki and pizza. Toppings are open season as vegan okonomiyaki comes from the Japanese words 'yaki' meaning 'cooked', 'okonomi' meaning 'as you like' and 'vegan' which is just an international term for 'picky eater'.

Combine the flaxseed meal and aquafaba or water in a bowl. Set aside to thicken for at least 5 minutes.

To make the okonomiyaki sauce, whisk the ingredients in a bowl and set aside.

Combine the cabbage, potato, spring onion and fried shallots in a large bowl.

In a separate bowl, mix the flour, vegetable stock and prepared flaxseed mixture, then pour this mixture over the vegetables. Using your hands, mix everything together really well – there won't be too much batter covering everything. Set aside for at least 15 minutes.

Heat 2 tablespoons of canola oil in a small frying pan over medium–low heat. Spoon one-quarter of the vegetable mixture into the pan and, using a spatula, press the mixture to the edge of the pan so it forms a pancake. Cook for about 5 minutes, then flip over and cook, adding a little extra oil if needed, for a further 5 minutes or until golden brown and crisp. Remove from the pan and keep warm while you cook the remaining okonomiyaki.

Drizzle a little of the okonomiyaki sauce over each pancake, along with some Japanese mayo. Scatter over pickled sushi ginger, shredded nori, a few fried shallots and finish with sliced spring onion.

Meat loather's pizza

Ingredients

olive oil, for brushing

60 g (2 oz/½ cup) shredded dairy-free
 cheese

250 g (9 oz) mixed faux meat of your
 choice, at room temperature

barbecue sauce, for drizzling

aioli, for drizzling

your favourite hot sauce, for drizzling

Pizza dough

1¼ teaspoons instant dried yeast

300 g (10½ oz/2 cups) Italian 00 flour,
 plus extra for dusting

2 teaspoons sea salt flakes

1 tablespoon olive oil, plus extra
 for greasing

Pizza sauce

400 g (14 oz) tin plum (roma) tomatoes

90 g (3 oz/⅓ cup) tomato paste
 (concentrated purée)

3 garlic cloves

1 teaspoon fennel seeds

1 teaspoon dried thyme

1 teaspoon dried oregano

½ teaspoon dried basil

1 teaspoon celery salt

½ teaspoon onion powder

¼ teaspoon chilli powder

½ teaspoon granulated sugar

½ teaspoon freshly ground black pepper

Find a mix of meat alternatives for this recipe. I like to combine pepperoni, pork sausage and shredded chicken. Even better, use the sausages and seitan chickpea chicken on pages 82 and 163 in this book!

If you're making the dough a few days in advance, increase the quantity of water to 200 ml (7 fl oz) and leave to prove in the fridge until required for a perfect dough.

To make the dough, combine 170 ml (5½ fl oz/⅔ cup) water and the yeast in a jug and set aside for 10 minutes or until frothy. You don't need to add sugar for the yeast to work, but adding a pinch of flour after a few minutes will give the yeast plenty of sugars to begin blooming.

Tip the flour into a large bowl and crumble in the salt flakes. Make a well in the middle and pour in the yeast mixture. Use a spatula to fold the flour into the liquid until you have a loose dough. Use your hands to form a dough ball and knead in the olive oil. Transfer to a lightly floured work surface and knead for 10 minutes or until the dough is smooth and elastic. Place the dough into a bowl lightly greased with oil, then cover and leave to prove for at least 1 hour.

Meanwhile, to make the pizza sauce, place all the ingredients in a blender and process to a smooth sauce. This sauce makes enough for four pizzas, so keep any left-over pizza sauce in an airtight container in the fridge for up to 1 week. During this time the sauce will thicken, so add a few splashes of water before using.

Preheat the oven to 260°C (500°F) or the highest temperature it will go and place a large baking tray or pizza tray in the oven to heat up.

Back to the dough. Lightly dust your work surface and a rolling pin with flour. Transfer just over half the dough to your work surface and roll out to a 26 cm (10¼ in) pizza base, dusting with flour and rotating the dough as you go. Round the edges off by folding them in and rolling back out until smooth. Carefully drag the pizza base onto a large square of baking paper. Wrap the remaining dough in plastic wrap and use to make the Pizza waffle on page 119.

Cover the pizza base with a generous helping of pizza sauce, leaving a border around the edge for the crust. Using a pastry brush, brush a little olive oil over the exposed crust. Scatter most of the cheese over the sauce, then randomly scatter the faux meat on top. Finish with the remaining cheese and a few extra blobs of pizza sauce for good luck.

Remove the hot baking tray or pizza tray from the oven and very carefully transfer the pizza and baking paper to the tray. Place on the top shelf of the oven and bake for 12–15 minutes, until the cheese is bubbling and brown spots appear on the base of the crust.

Remove the pizza from the oven and douse in barbecue sauce, aioli and hot sauce. Cut into eight slices and serve immediately.

Korean spicy fried 'chicken'

Ingredients

700 g (1 lb 9 oz) steamed Seitan chickpea
    chicken (see page 163 or use store-
    bought), cut into 5 cm x 2.5 cm
    (2 in x 1 in) irregular chunks
2 teaspoons minced ginger
2 teaspoons soy sauce
canola oil, for deep-frying
sea salt
thinly sliced spring onion (scallion),
    to serve
toasted sesame seeds, for sprinkling

Coating

60 g (2 oz/½ cup) potato starch
40 g (1½ oz) plain (all-purpose) flour
35 g (1¼ oz) cornflour (corn starch)
1 teaspoon baking powder
1 teaspoon freshly ground black pepper
1 teaspoon sea salt

Sauce

6 garlic cloves, minced
95 g (3¼ oz) gochujang, plus extra to taste
55 ml (1¾ fl oz) tomato ketchup
3 tablespoons Vegan honey (see page 170)
    or rice malt syrup
4 teaspoons white vinegar

This recipe might be a little time intensive to make from scratch, but one could argue that it takes a lot less time than raising a chicken. Opting for store-bought seitan or faux chicken and rice malt syrup brings the preparation for this recipe down to less than 30 minutes.

Combine the seitan chunks, ginger and soy sauce in a large bowl until the ginger is distributed evenly and the seitan has absorbed the soy sauce.

In a separate bowl, combine the coating ingredients. Add the seitan, toss to coat and set aside for 10 minutes.

Meanwhile, heat the canola oil in a large saucepan or deep-fryer to 180°C (350°F) using a kitchen thermometer to assist you.

Toss the seitan pieces again in any remaining coating mixture to achieve a dry exterior. Place immediately into the hot oil and fry for 3–4 minutes to cook through. If the seitan pieces are browning too quickly, remove from the pan and allow to cool before flash-frying again until crisp. Transfer to a plate lined with paper towel to drain and sprinkle with salt.

While the seitan is frying, make the sauce. Fry the garlic in a small saucepan with 1 teaspoon of the hot frying oil over medium heat for 2 minutes. Add the remaining sauce ingredients and simmer, stirring occasionally, until the sauce starts to follow the spoon about, adding a splash of water if you want to make it runnier. This should be ready by the time you take the seitan out of the oil. Taste and add an extra squeeze of gochujang if your friends can handle it.

Put the finishing touches on your masterpiece by using a pastry brush to paint the sauce onto the surface of the fried seitan, brushing as much flavour as you can into the crevices. Or, less artfully, dump the seitan into a bowl and pour the sauce over the top, tossing until fully coated.

Serve with thinly sliced spring onion and toasted sesame seeds scattered over the top.

Tex-Mex tacos

Ingredients

canola oil, for deep-frying
4 corn tortillas
60 g (2 oz/¼ cup) Salsa (see page 38
    or use store-bought)
¼ iceberg lettuce, shredded
1 tomato, chopped
Sour cream (see page 169), to serve
guacamole, to serve

Taco seasoning

1 teaspoon chilli powder
⅓ teaspoon smoked paprika
½ teaspoon ground cumin
⅛ teaspoon ground coriander
½ teaspoon dried oregano
¼ teaspoon garlic powder
¼ teaspoon onion powder
½ teaspoon sea salt
⅛ teaspoon freshly ground black pepper

Taco mince

2 tablespoons canola oil
1 small red or brown onion, thinly sliced
250 g (9 oz) mixed mushrooms,
    roughly chopped
1 teaspoon beef-style stock powder
120 g (4½ oz) TVP (Textured Vegetable
    Protein) mince
2 tablespoons tomato paste
    (concentrated purée)
2 teaspoons liquid smoke
1 teaspoon molasses

This recipe calls for liquid smoke and molasses. If you don't have these ingredients on hand, I guess you'll be eating something else for dinner. Just kidding! Simply substitute barbecue sauce instead.

To make the taco seasoning, combine the ingredients in a small bowl and set aside.

To make the taco mince, heat the canola oil in a large saucepan over medium heat. Add the onion and sauté for 5 minutes, then add the mushroom and cook for a further 5 minutes or until the mixture starts to catch on the base of the pan. Pour in 250 ml (8½ fl oz/1 cup) water, along with the beef-style stock and deglaze the pan. Remove from the heat and use a stick blender to pulse the mixture until smooth.

Return the pan to the heat and add the TVP, stirring until all the liquid has been absorbed. Add the tomato paste, liquid smoke and molasses and stir through. Cook over medium heat for 5 minutes, stirring, then add 2 teaspoons of the taco seasoning. Taste and add more taco seasoning if desired. Stir occasionally for 2 minutes, then remove from the heat once the spices are aromatic.

Heat the oil in a large heavy-based saucepan over medium–high heat. Test if the oil is ready by inserting a wooden skewer or the handle of a wooden spoon into the oil; if it begins to bubble quickly then you're ready to go.

One by one, place the corn tortillas into the hot frying oil. After 15 seconds, use tongs to flip each tortilla and carefully fold it into a hard taco shell, holding it in place for a further 20 seconds until crisp, then set aside on a plate lined with paper towel to drain.

Divide the salsa, lettuce, tomato and taco mince among the taco shells and serve with sour cream and guacamole on the side to smear over the top.

Loaded baked potatoes

Ingredients

8 small or 4 large all-purpose potatoes

olive oil, for brushing

sea salt flakes

4 spring onions (scallions), finely chopped, white and green parts separated

75 g (2¾ oz) pickled jalapenos, minced

8 sheets crispy Rice paper bacon (see page 164), roughly chopped into small pieces (reserve the prettiest pieces for garnish)

1 tablespoon Rice paper bacon marinade (see page 164)

freshly ground black pepper, to taste

125 g (4½ oz/1 cup) shredded dairy-free cheese

smoked paprika, for sprinkling

Sour cream (see page 169), to serve

snipped chives, to serve

Sophia Loren's tip for perfect skin as you age is to add olive oil to your bath. Elevate this with my bonus tip: brush potatoes with salt and olive oil before baking. Meanwhile, experience the same treatment by running a bath with bath salts and a glug of olive oil. Emerge over an hour later with radiant skin and freshly baked potato ready to go.

Preheat the oven to 180°C (350°F).

Use a fork to stab the potatoes all over so that steam can escape. Brush the potatoes with olive oil and coat in fat salt flakes. Bake directly on an oven shelf, rotating 2–3 times, for 1–2 hours, depending on the size of your potatoes. Your potatoes are ready when the skins are crisp and a fork easily slides through the flesh. (You can also blast your potatoes in batches of four in the microwave for up to 10 minutes on high and then bake at 200°C/400°F for about 30 minutes or until soft if you're in a rush.)

Remove the potatoes from the oven and cut the tops off to allow steam to escape (keep these little hats!). Once cool enough to handle, use a teaspoon to carefully scoop out the flesh into a bowl while leaving the skins intact.

Add the white spring onion, jalapeno, rice paper bacon, marinade, pepper and three-quarters of the shredded cheese to the potato flesh and gently mash to combine. Scoop the potato mixture back into the potato skins and scatter the remaining cheese on top. Place the stuffed potatoes and their hats on a baking tray and return to the oven for 25 minutes or until the cheese is bubbling.

Remove the loaded potatoes from the oven and top with the green spring onion and a sprinkling of smoked paprika. Rest the hats on the loaded potatoes and position the reserved rice paper bacon on top. Serve with a dollop of sour cream on the side and a pinch of freshly snipped chives.

Sofritas burrito bowl

Serves 4

Ingredients

½ teaspoon sea salt

200 g (7 oz/1 cup) medium-grain
white rice, rinsed

60 g (2 oz/½ cup) shredded
dairy-free cheddar

15 g (½ oz/¼ cup) nutritional yeast

½ teaspoon ground cumin

splash of olive oil

400 g (14 oz) tin sweetcorn kernels, rinsed
and drained

420 g (15 oz) tin black beans, rinsed
and drained

1 teaspoon Taco seasoning (see page 112)

1 avocado, sliced

1 lime, quartered

4 coriander (cilantro) sprigs,
to serve (optional)

Chipotle mayonnaise

1 x quantity Mayonnaise (see page 165 or
use store-bought vegan mayonnaise)

2 chipotles in adobo sauce, finely chopped

1 tablespoon adobo sauce

1 teaspoon freshly squeezed lime juice

½ teaspoon garlic powder

Sofritas

½ green capsicum (bell pepper), deseeded

1 tomato, roughly chopped

1–2 chipotles in adobo sauce

3 garlic cloves

2 tablespoons adobo sauce

1½ tablespoons soy sauce

1 tablespoon olive oil

1½ teaspoons freshly squeezed lime juice

1 teaspoon onion powder

⅓ teaspoon ground cumin

¼ teaspoon dried oregano

¼ teaspoon sea salt

pinch of freshly ground black pepper

300 g (10½ oz) firm tofu

One might assume a burrito bowl is deviating from the junk-food theme of this book and starting to err on the healthy side. You'll be glad to hear this bowl calls for melted cheese throughout the rice base, marinated tofu and a chipotle mayonnaise so moreish you probably won't even notice what's underneath it anyway.

To make the chipotle mayonnaise, combine the ingredients in a small bowl. Set aside in the fridge until needed.

To make the sofritas, preheat a grill (broiler) to high. Grill the capsicum, skin side up, for 10 minutes or until starting to char. Transfer to a food processor along with the remaining sofritas ingredients except the tofu. Process until smooth and thick, then transfer to a large bowl.

Wrap the tofu in paper towel, place a heavy weight on top and leave it to chill out for 20 minutes. Unwrap the tofu, wipe away the excess moisture, then cut it into thick slices. Stab the tofu all over with a fork, then toss it in the sofritas and set aside to marinate.

Place 375 ml (12½ fl oz/1½ cups) water and the salt in a saucepan and bring to the boil over high heat. Add the rice, then cover and reduce the heat to a simmer. Cook for 13 minutes or until the liquid has evaporated. Remove the pan from the heat and fluff the rice with a fork. Stir through the cheese, nutritional yeast and cumin. Divide the rice among four serving bowls and keep warm.

Heat the olive oil in a small frying pan over high heat. Add the corn and sauté for 5 minutes or until the corn starts to char. Add the black beans and taco seasoning and cook for 2 minutes or until fragrant. Transfer the mixture to a bowl and place the pan back over the heat.

Remove the tofu from the marinade and place it in the pan, searing for 2–3 minutes on both sides. Once the tofu begins to brown, use a spatula to break the tofu into small chunks. Pour in the sofritas, reduce the heat to medium and cook for 10 minutes or until heated through. Spoon the sofritas and tofu over one-quarter of the cheesy rice and divide the black bean mixture and avocado over the remainder of the rice.

Heap chipotle mayonnaise on top of each bowl. Rest a lime quarter on top, along with a sprig of coriander (if using) to impress your Instagram followers before photographing and serving.

Pizza waffle

Ingredients

plain (all-purpose) flour, for dusting
½ quantity Pizza dough (see
    pages 108–109)
cooking oil spray
60 ml (2 fl oz/¼ cup) Pizza sauce,
    plus extra, warm, to serve (see
    pages 108–109)
25 g (¾ oz) pitted black olives,
    thinly sliced
¼ small red onion, thinly sliced
30 g (1 oz) sliced vegan pepperoni or
    Rice paper bacon (see page 164)
1 dairy-free cheese slice

A calzone in drag, feeling its waffle fantasy. Elevate the look of this dish by replacing the pepperoni with rice paper bacon on the outside of the dough to create waffled-in bacon strips for a reveal at the end that could only be beaten if you'd stuffed the whole thing with rose petals.

Roll out the dough on a floured work surface as thinly as possible. Use a waffle iron to lightly press two waffle shapes into the dough, then cut out two rectangles larger than the size of the waffle iron.

Thoroughly spray the waffle iron with cooking oil spray and set over a medium stovetop flame to heat on one side before flipping and heating the other side. Once the waffle iron is sizzling hot, carefully place one of the dough rectangles onto the iron and cook for 3 minutes.

While the dough is cooking, smear on the pizza sauce, leaving a 1 cm (½ in) edge and scatter over the olives, onion and pepperoni or bacon. Place the remaining dough rectangle on top to completely enclose the filling.

Remove the waffle iron from the flame and hold it over the sink. Close and lock the waffle iron, then thank me for warning you to do this over the sink. Press down firmly. Use a knife to trim any excess filling that has squeezed out, then flip the waffle iron and return it to the heat.

When steam starts to escape, flip and open the iron to release. Close again and continue cooking and flipping for 12–14 minutes, until both sides of the waffle are crisp. Keep your eye on the waffle at all times and hold it over the sink as needed if the filling tries to bubble out. When one side has crisped, flip and open the iron. Lay the cheese slice on top and allow to melt as the other side finishes crisping.

Remove the pizza waffle from the iron and serve hot with extra pizza sauce for dipping.

Gnocchi with kale chip pesto

Ingredients

1 kg (2 lb 3 oz) potatoes
110 g (4 oz/¾ cup) Italian 00 flour, plus
    extra for dusting
½ teaspoon sea salt, plus extra to taste
3 tablespoons dairy-free butter
freshly ground black pepper
juice of 1 lemon
nutritional yeast, for sprinkling
125 g (4½ oz/1 cup) shredded
    dairy-free cheese

Kale chip pesto

1 large bunch kale, leaves stripped
125 ml (4 fl oz/½ cup) olive oil, plus extra
    for drizzling (get the good stuff out for
    this one)
1 teaspoon sea salt
2 bunches basil, small stalks and
    leaves picked
15 g (½ oz/¼ cup) nutritional yeast
juice of 1 lemon, plus extra if desired
2 garlic cloves
80 g (2¾ oz/½ cup) raw cashews or
    60 g (2 oz/½ cup) sunflower seeds

Not a fan of kale? Well, it's not so fond of you either. Try to put your differences aside and give it another go baked, then turned into pesto and tossed over freshly cooked, pan-fried gnocchi. If you can't learn to love it in this form, there's no hope for reconciliation.

Preheat the oven to 180°C (350°F). Line two baking trays with baking paper.

Use a fork to stab the potatoes all over so that steam can escape. Bake directly on an oven shelf, rotating 2–3 times, for 1–2 hours, depending on the size of your potatoes. They are ready when the skins are crisp and the insides are soft. (You can also blast your potatoes in the microwave for 10 minutes on high and then bake at 200°C/400°F for 30 minutes or until soft if you're in a rush.)

Meanwhile, to make the kale chip pesto, place the kale leaves in a bowl, drizzle over a glug of olive oil and sprinkle in the salt. Massage the oil and salt into the leaves, then place on the prepared trays in a single layer. Bake in the oven until the leaves crisp up but remove them before they go dark brown. This can take anywhere from 10 to 18 minutes, so keep a close eye on them.

Place the kale and remaining pesto ingredients except the cashews or sunflower seeds in a food processor and pulse several times, scraping down the side of the bowl as needed. Add the cashews or sunflower seeds and process until combined, but with visible pieces of cashew or sunflower seed still showing. If you would like a runnier consistency, add extra olive oil or lemon juice.

Remove the potatoes from the oven and immediately cut in half to allow steam to escape. While hot, use a teaspoon to carefully scoop the flesh into a potato ricer, then rice the potato into a bowl. You can also do this with two forks, but it's important not to mash the potato as it needs to be light and fluffy. You should end up with around 500 g (1 lb 2 oz) of potato.

While the potato is still warm, use your hands to gradually mix in the flour and salt until you achieve a smooth dough. Transfer to a floured work surface.

Using your hands, roll the dough into a long 2 cm (¾ in) wide log, lightly flouring as you go. Use a knife to cut the log into small 2–3 cm (¾ in–1¼ in) gnocchi. Roll the gnocchi into small balls and use your finger to create a little indent in each of the balls to catch the pesto. No two pieces should look the same.

Bring a stockpot of heavily salted water to a simmer over medium–high heat. Do not boil! Add the gnocchi a handful at a time to the pan and cook for 1–2 minutes, or until the gnocchi float to the surface. Using a slotted spoon, remove to a colander to drain.

Place the butter in a large frying pan and set over high heat. Add the drained gnocchi and fry for 3–5 minutes on one side until golden. Flip and repeat on the other side. Season the gnocchi with salt and pepper, then pour in the lemon juice, sprinkle over a good amount of nutritional yeast and toss through the shredded cheese while it's hot. Remove from the heat, stir through enough kale chip pesto to coat and serve warm.

Any left-over pesto will keep in an airtight container in the fridge for 3–4 days.

Kakiage

Ingredients

1 onion, thinly sliced
1 small sweet potato, cut into thin matchsticks
2–3 carrots, cut into thin matchsticks
100 g (3½ oz) green beans, trimmed and sliced lengthways
12 shiso leaves
fried shallots
150 g (5½ oz/1 cup) plain (all-purpose) flour
60 g (2 oz/½ cup) cornflour (corn starch) or potato starch
large pinch of sea salt
40 g (1½ oz) Japanese mayonnaise (see page 165), plus extra to serve
canola oil, for shallow-frying
soy sauce and teriyaki sauce, to serve

Give those sad-looking vegetables at the back of your fridge a new identity by frying them in a crispy batter until they're unrecognisable. This recipe is one of my go-to dinner dishes and it's definitely my favourite way to clean the fridge. Eat on its own, over rice, or use as a sushi filling.

Place the vegetables, shiso leaves and fried shallots in a large bowl.

In a small bowl, combine the flour, cornflour and salt. Sprinkle about 1 tablespoon of the flour mixture over the vegetable mixture, stirring until the ingredients are coated in a thin, floury layer.

In a larger bowl, combine 250 ml (8½ fl oz/1 cup) ice-cold water with the mayonnaise (the oil-based mayonnaise in the batter will fizzle away as it fries, leading to an extra-crispy finish). Add the remaining flour mixture to the mayonnaise mixture and gently stir (as little as you can), just until the flour is loosely mixed in.

Pour the batter over the vegetable mixture and lightly stir to just coat the ingredients.

Heat enough canola oil for shallow-frying in a large heavy-based frying pan over medium–high heat. Test if the oil is ready by inserting a wooden skewer or the handle of a wooden spoon into the oil; if it begins to bubble quickly then you're ready to go.

Working in batches, use a spatula and a spoon to prepare each kakiage for frying. Spoon your desired amount of battered ingredients onto a spatula before lowering the spatula into the hot oil and using the spoon to scrape it off into the oil. Cook on one side for 3 minutes or until it is crisp enough to flip without falling apart, then cook the other side for a further 3 minutes. Remove from the oil and drain on a plate lined with paper towel.

Transfer the kakiage to a serving plate and drizzle over a good amount of Japanese mayo, soy sauce and teriyaki sauce.

Don't be limited by the vegetables listed here; you can also use sliced eggplant (aubergine), broccoli florets and shiitake mushrooms. Use whatever you have to hand!

Herb-stuffed cheese quesadillas

Ingredients

4 spring onions (scallions), thinly sliced

⅓ red capsicum (bell pepper), cut into small dice

2 bird's eye chillies, roughly chopped

2 bunches basil, small stalks and leaves very finely chopped

1½ bunches coriander (cilantro), small stalks and leaves very finely chopped

¼ bunch mint, small stalks and leaves very finely chopped

olive oil, for cooking

8 corn tortillas or 4 large wheat tortillas

250 ml (8½ fl oz/1 cup) Cashew queso dip without salsa (see page 38)

40 g (1½ oz) shredded dairy-free cheese

1 lime, cut into wedges

sliced avocado, Sour cream (see page 169) and hot sauce, to serve

Unfortunately, some people are genetically inferior and cannot enjoy the wonders of coriander. With luck, their genes will have been bred out within a few generations, but until then they'll just have to miss out on this awesome recipe. This dish is my childhood favourite: my father's interpretation of quesadillas which I've further bastardised by making vegan. Double the recipe for celebrations to serve at a banquet feast, alongside a share plate of charred-up meat alternatives.

Combine the spring onion, capsicum, chilli and herbs in a large bowl.

Heat a little olive oil in a large frying pan over medium heat. Place a tortilla in the pan and smear either one-eighth or one-quarter of the cashew queso dip (depending on whether you are using corn or wheat tortillas) over the surface, leaving a 2 cm (¾ in) border. Add either one-eighth or one-quarter of the herb mixture over the cashew queso dip and scatter the same quantity of shredded cheese over the top to work like glue.

Place another tortilla over the cheese and use a spatula to press down firmly and evenly, pushing the filling out to meet the edge of the tortilla, but stopping before it tumbles out. Check the base of your tortilla and adjust the heat if needed – you don't want the tortilla to start browning before the filling has had a chance to heat through. Cook the tortilla until the base starts to turn golden and the cheese begins to melt, then brush the top tortilla with a little oil, slide your spatula underneath the quesadilla with your fingers placed on top and flip! Now cook the underside until crisp and the filling is nicely melted. This whole process can take over 10 minutes, so patience is a virtue. (If flipping is out of your comfort zone, you can build the quesadilla by filling half of the tortilla and folding it over; this way, you get twice the amount of quesadillas – nice!) Repeat with the remaining tortillas and filling.

Use kitchen scissors or a pizza cutter to cut the quesadillas into slices. Squeeze fresh lime juice over the top and serve with sliced avocado, sour cream and your favourite hot sauce.

SWEETS

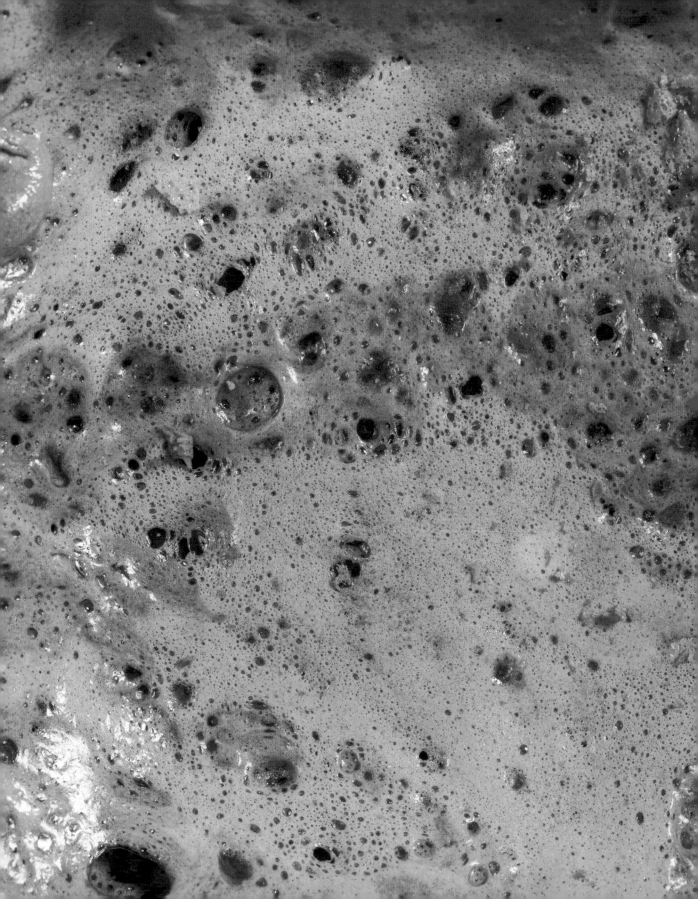

There's scarcely a fruit to be found in this chapter; we've moved them to the meat-alternative recipes so they wouldn't be confused as healthy. The bananas from the usual vegan ice-cream recipes have been removed and deep-fried instead. The ice creams make investing in a cheap ice-cream maker more appealing than ever with chocolate hazelnut, chai or an ice cream made with Hershey's syrup and sandwiched between two cookies. Alternatively, make your own honey from scratch, then turn it into chocolate-covered honeycomb or baklava fro-yo.

We don't pretend a tin of coconut milk tastes exactly like whipped cream, and the jewel of Australian desserts – fablova – tastes all the better for it. The silky, soft centre that's a must for a proper pavlova hasn't been forgotten and, fine, there's a bit of fruit on top, too. If you prefer something warm don't turn your deep-fryer off yet. You'll want to flick to the syrup-drenched Greek doughnuts (loukoumades) or the beer-battered chocolate bars.

These sweets might be vegan, but they're no healthy knockoff. In this chapter we do it right and don't shy away from good things like fat and sugar. Take your scales out of the bathroom and move them into the kitchen, it's dessert time.

Loukoumades

Ingredients

2 teaspoons instant dried yeast
300 g (10½ oz/2 cups) plain
   (all-purpose) flour
½ teaspoon sea salt
canola oil, for deep-frying, plus extra
   for coating
Vegan honey (see page 170), for drizzling
unsalted shelled pistachios, crushed,
   for sprinkling

Greek doughnuts are satisfyingly simple to make. Drowning them in vegan honey once they're fried is the only golden rule. For a truly authentic serving suggestion, don't make them at all and instead invite around Greek friends or relatives. Trust that they'll be bringing loukoumades, alongside a cornucopia of other food you never asked for and a list of questions as to why you don't have a partner yet.

Combine the yeast and 125 ml (4 fl oz/½ cup) warm water in a small jug and set aside for 10 minutes or until the mixture becomes frothy. You don't need to add sugar for the yeast to work, but adding a pinch of flour after a few minutes will give the yeast plenty of sugars to begin blooming.

Place the flour and salt in a large bowl and stir to combine. Make a well in the centre and add the yeast mixture and 185 ml (6½ fl oz/¾ cup) water. Using a wooden spoon, bring the mixture together until you have a sticky and relatively runny dough. Cover with plastic wrap and set aside in a warm spot for at least 1 hour, until doubled in size.

Heat the canola oil in a large heavy-based saucepan over medium–high heat. Test if the oil is ready by inserting a wooden skewer or the handle of a wooden spoon into the oil; if it begins to bubble quickly then you're ready to go.

Here's where it can get messy. Pour a little oil into a cup. Dip a metal dessertspoon into the oil, then use it to scoop out a spoonful of the dough mixture (the oil will make it easier for the dough to slide off). Use your finger to quickly slide the dough from the spoon into the hot oil. Aim for the most fluid motion you can, while also not dropping the loukoumades batter from too high into the oil. These factors will determine how round your doughnuts will be.

Working in small batches, fry the loukoumades for 1–2 minutes, using a slotted spoon to turn them in the oil. They will cook very fast so keep a keen eye on them. Once the loukoumades have an even golden coating, scoop them out and drain on a plate lined with paper towel.

Place the warm loukoumades on a serving plate, drizzle over an unhealthy amount of honey and sprinkle with pistachios. Serve immediately.

Tiramousse

Ingredients

2½ tablespoons instant coffee
100 g (3½ oz) caster (superfine) sugar
4 teaspoons pure icing
  (confectioners') sugar
2 teaspoons natural vanilla extract
cocoa powder, for dusting
vegan dark chocolate, for grating

Cream

155 g (5½ oz/1 cup) raw cashews
60 ml (2 fl oz/¼ cup) maple syrup
½ teaspoon natural vanilla extract
1 tablespoon coconut yoghurt
½ teaspoon lactic acid

Base

200 g (7 oz) your favourite vegan
  chocolate cookies
50 ml (1¾ fl oz) melted dairy-free butter
2 tablespoons dark rum
pinch of sea salt flakes

Tiramousse is so rich, you'll expect it to pick up the bill at the end of dinner. Serve at the end of a dinner party to give your guests an extra boost of energy to get out of your house so you can go to bed.

To make the base, in a food processor or by smashing in a zip-lock bag with a rolling pin, crush the cookies. Transfer to a bowl and stir in the butter, rum and salt until combined.

To make the cream, blend the cashews, maple syrup, vanilla, coconut yoghurt and lactic acid in a blender. Prepare your four most beautiful and potentially breakable glasses for serving in.

Combine the coffee, caster sugar and 60 ml (2 fl oz/¼ cup) water in a large, clean metal bowl. Use electric beaters to beat for 5 minutes. You'll need the full 5 minutes to get over the shock that this is actually turning into coffee cream. Sift in the icing sugar and vanilla and beat until fully incorporated and the cream is thick.

Divide the base mixture among the glasses and press into the bottom. Layer half the coffee cream on top, followed by all of the cream. Dust cocoa powder over the top.

Pour over the other half of the coffee cream and smooth the surface. Grate a little dark chocolate over the top, but do not dust with extra cocoa powder.

Set aside in the fridge until dessert time.

Chocolate ice cream and peanut butter cookie sandwiches

Ingredients

50 (1¾ oz/¼ cup) vegetable shortening
110 g (4 oz) dairy-free butter
110 g (4 oz/½ cup) granulated sugar
110 g (4 oz/½ cup) brown sugar
3 tablespoons aquafaba
60 g (2 oz/¼ cup) smooth peanut butter
1 teaspoon natural vanilla extract
150 g (5½ oz/1 cup) plain (all-purpose) flour
30 g (1 oz/¼ cup) cornflour (corn starch)
¾ teaspoon bicarbonate of soda
   (baking soda)
1 teaspoon sea salt

Chocolate ice cream

465 ml (15½ fl oz) soy milk
250 g (9 oz/¾ cup) Hershey's syrup
pinch of guar gum or xanthan gum
1 tablespoon natural vanilla extract
1 tablespoon dark rum or vodka
½ teaspoon instant coffee
½ teaspoon sea salt
30 g (1 oz) vegan dark chocolate
1 tablespoon freshly squeezed lemon juice
50 g (1¾ oz/½ cup) soy milk powder
55 g (2 oz/¼ cup) coconut oil
2 tablespoons sunflower oil

Some ice-cream sandwich recipes try to convince you that they're best served with cookies fresh from the oven. This is probably because they don't know how to properly freeze their cookies. Try this recipe where your sandwiches can sit patiently in the freezer until you remember you left them there.

To make the chocolate ice cream, place 280 ml (9½ fl oz) of the soy milk, the Hershey's syrup, gum, vanilla, rum or vodka, coffee and salt in a small saucepan and bring to a simmer over medium heat. Crumble in the dark chocolate and stir until melted. Transfer to a large bowl and set aside to cool.

Place the remaining soy milk, the lemon juice, soy milk powder, coconut oil and sunflower oil in a blender and blend until well combined. Add in the cooled Hershey's syrup mixture and blend until completely combined. Transfer to the fridge for at least 6 hours, or until fully cold.

Transfer the chilled chocolate mixture to an ice-cream machine and churn according to the manufacturer's instructions for 25–30 minutes. Place the ice cream in an airtight container and smooth the surface with a spatula. Freeze for several hours until firm.

Preheat the oven to 160°C (320°F). Line a baking tray with baking paper.

Place the shortening, butter and both the sugars in a large bowl. Using electric beaters, beat until creamy, then add the aquafaba and beat until incorporated. Beat in the peanut butter and vanilla.

In a separate bowl, combine the flour, cornflour, bicarb soda and salt. Beat this into the butter and sugar mixture a little at a time until everything comes together.

Form the cookie batter into 12 small balls and place on the prepared tray. They will spread as they bake so leave them plenty of personal space.

Bake for 12–16 minutes, then remove from the oven and set aside to completely cool. Once cool, transfer the cookies to the freezer, until you're ready to build your sandwiches.

Remove the ice cream from the freezer and scoop a ball of ice cream onto a cookie. Place another cookie on top and use a knife to smooth the edge of the ice cream so it's flush with the cookies. Wrap up tightly in plastic wrap and return to the freezer to firm up. Repeat the process to make six ice-cream sandwiches.

Inhale.

Cookies and cream cheesecake

Ingredients

32 Oreos

3 tablespoons coconut oil

4 teaspoons agar agar powder

75 ml (2½ fl oz) hot water

125 ml (4 fl oz/½ cup) dairy-free
   condensed milk

500 g (1 lb 2 oz/2 cups) Cream cheese
   (see page 169)

35 g (1¼ oz) pure icing
   (confectioners') sugar

1 teaspoon natural vanilla extract

This recipes borrows concepts from the most popular of non-vegan desserts, which seem to usually just be store-bought desserts combined and presented as a new dish. This fool-proof combination of cookies and cream cheese works whether you purchase readily available dairy-free cream cheese for ease or try the recipe from this book for the cheesy undertones that make this taste like a proper cheesecake.

Twist and scrape the cream from 16 of the Oreos and place in a bowl, then crush the 16 creamless Oreo biscuits in a food processor or smash them to crumbs in a zip-lock bag with a rolling pin. Transfer to a bowl.

Melt the coconut oil in a small saucepan over low heat, then pour the oil over the crushed Oreos and mix well to completely combine. Press the mixture into the bottom and side of an 18 cm (7 in) cake tin, to create your cheesecake base. Set aside in the freezer while you proceed with the next step.

To make the filling, in a large bowl, stir the agar agar rapidly into the hot water until combined. Add the condensed milk, cream cheese, left-over Oreo cream, icing sugar and vanilla and stir. Crush the remaining Oreos using your chosen smashing method, stopping while they're still chunky and not too fine. Stir them through.

Pour the filling into the prepared crust, smooth the top with a spatula, then return the cheesecake to the freezer for 6 hours or until completely set. At this point, it is ready to eat and will stay ready to slice and serve straight from the freezer.

Fablova

Ingredients

vinegar, for dabbing
125 ml (4 fl oz/½ cup) chilled aquafaba
¼ teaspoon cream of tartar
120 g (4½ oz) caster (superfine) sugar
¼ teaspoon xanthan gum

Filling

¼ teaspoon cream of tartar
125 ml (4 fl oz/½ cup) chilled aquafaba
230 g (8 oz/1 cup) caster (sueprfine) sugar
2¼ teaspoons agar agar powder
80 ml (2½ fl oz/⅓ cup) glucose syrup
½ teaspoon xanthan gum
2 teaspoons natural vanilla extract

Topping

250 g (9 oz) can soy or rice whip
fresh strawberries, kiwi fruit, mango
    and passionfruit

Pavlova is an Australian and Kiwi classic comprising a silky-soft filling and meringue-like crust, topped with whipped cream and fruit that's perfect for Christmas. If your experience of vegan pavlova has been a brick of meringue hidden under coconut cream, you've been wronged and you must try this truer-to-life version instead.

Preheat the oven to 110°C (230°F). If you and your oven have an untrustworthy relationship, it doesn't cost much to invest in an oven thermometer, especially when working at fiddly low temperatures such as for this recipe.

Use a paper towel dabbed with vinegar to wipe out a large metal bowl and the attachments on your electric beaters. Pour the aquafaba into the bowl and add the cream of tartar. Beat on high speed for 5 minutes. It will bubble, froth and foam, and then turn into soft peaks much like meringue.

Turn the beaters to medium and add the sugar 1 tablespoon at a time, incorporating each tablespoon into the meringue before adding the next. At the end the meringue should have formed stiff peaks. Mix in the xanthan gum and beat on high for another minute. The meringue is ready when it doesn't budge when you flip the bowl upside down.

Line two large baking trays with baking paper. Use a marker to trace the shape of a 23 cm (9 in) cake tin onto each piece of paper, flipping the paper over once done. Spoon the prepared meringue mixture inside the traced circles (it will expand very slightly), piling up and smoothing out until you have two discs.

Place the baking trays on the middle and top shelves in the oven and dry the meringues (we're not trying to bake them) for 3 hours or until the tops feel crisp. Switch off the oven, leave the door closed and forget about them until they're completely cool.

While the crusts are drying, make the filling. Beat the cream of tartar and aquafaba until you achieve soft peaks again and set aside. Heat the sugar and agar agar powder in a saucepan over medium–low heat and stir in 170 ml (5½ fl oz/⅔ cup) water and the glucose syrup. Using a candy thermometer to guide you, and without stirring, bring the temperature to 110°C (230°F). Between 100°C (212°F) and 110°C (230°F) the mixture will rise quickly, so be vigilant with the heat to coax it to the right temperature without the mixture flowing out of the pan. Give it a stir once done.

Slowly pour the sugar mixture into the whipped aquafaba, beating to incorporate as you go. Once done, beat in the xanthan gum and vanilla. Spoon the warm, beaten mixture into your cake tin and leave to cool to room temperature, then move to the fridge until needed.

When all the components are ready, up-end one of the cooled meringues onto a serving dish. Use a knife to separate the set filling from the side of the tin and carefully guide it onto the upside down meringue.

Top with the second meringue, trimming the filling in line with the meringue if needed. Shake and spray the whipped cream over the top of the fablova. Slice and arrange the fruit to cover the cream – go for abundance! The clock on the crispness of the meringue starts ticking as soon as you add the cream, so serve immediately.

Deep-fried banana fritters

Ingredients

canola oil, for deep-frying

130 g (4½ oz/¾ cup) rice flour

50 g (1¾ oz) desiccated or shredded
    coconut, plus extra to serve

2 tablespoons cornflour (corn starch),
    plus extra if needed

1 teaspoon natural vanilla extract

½ teaspoon bicarbonate of soda
    (baking soda)

¼ teaspoon sea salt

6 lady finger bananas

cinnamon sugar or pure icing
    (confectioners') sugar, for dusting

vegan caramel sauce, to serve

soy or rice whip, to serve

chopped unsalted peanuts, to serve

Many ingredients respond well to deep-frying, requiring only a simple batter for crispy results. Bananas are not one of those ingredients. This batter calls for rice flour, cornflour, dried coconut and bicarb soda for our best shot at a crunch before you hit the warm, gooey banana.

Heat the canola oil in a large heavy-based saucepan over medium–high heat. Test if the oil is ready by inserting a wooden skewer or the handle of a wooden spoon into the oil; if it begins to bubble quickly then you're ready to go.

Combine the rice flour, coconut, cornflour, vanilla extract, bicarb soda and sea salt in a bowl. While stirring, add up to 185 ml (6½ fl oz/¾ cup) cold water until you have a thick batter (you may not need all the water). If you need to thicken the batter so that it better clings to the banana, add in a little extra cornflour.

One by one, add the bananas to the batter and completely coat. Using a fork, lift the bananas out of the batter and carefully lower into the hot oil. Fry the bananas for up to 3 minutes or until golden and completely crisp. Transfer to a plate lined with paper towel to drain.

Sprinkle cinnamon sugar or icing sugar into a bowl, then toss the warm bananas in the sugar until coated.

Divide the bananas among serving plates and top with generous amounts of caramel sauce, soy or rice whip, shredded coconut and a few chopped peanuts.

Chocolate hazelnut ice cream

Makes about 1 litre (34 fl oz/4 cups)

Ingredients

500 ml (17 fl oz/2 cups) soy milk
½ x quantity Chocolate hazelnut spread
   (see page 171)
1½ tablespoons rum or vodka
2 teaspoons cocoa powder
½ teaspoon instant coffee
1½ tablespoons natural vanilla extract
½ teaspoon sea salt
pinch of guar gum or xanthan gum
1 tablespoon freshly squeezed lemon juice
2 tablespoons soy milk powder
55 g (2 oz/¼ cup) coconut oil
2 tablespoons sunflower oil
waffle cones, to serve
finely chopped hazelnuts, to serve

Vegan chocolate spread alternatives usually incorporate healthy ingredients that have no business being there. Raw cacao? No. Maple syrup? Try again. Stevia? Get the hell out. Go all in and try this full-bodied version of the beloved classic, turned into ice cream.

Place 280 ml (9½ fl oz) of the soy milk, two-thirds of the chocolate hazelnut spread, the rum or vodka, cocoa powder, coffee, vanilla, salt and gum in a blender and blitz until smooth. Transfer to a large bowl and set aside.

Add the remaining soy milk, the lemon juice, soy milk powder, coconut oil and sunflower oil to the blender and blend until well combined.

Pour the prepared chocolate hazelnut mixture back into the blender and blend again. Set the mixture aside in the fridge for at least 6 hours, until fully cold.

Transfer the chilled mixture to an ice-cream machine and churn according to the manufacturer's instructions for 25–30 minutes. Pour the ice cream into a freezer-friendly container and swirl in the remaining chocolate hazelnut spread. Cover the surface of the ice cream with plastic wrap and make sure the container is airtight to avoid ice crystals forming.

Freeze overnight, then scoop into waffle cones, sprinkle chopped hazelnuts over the top and serve.

Baklava

Ingredients

180 g (6½ oz/½ cup) Vegan honey
    (see page 170)
220 g (8 oz/1 cup) granulated sugar
zest of 1 lemon or orange (optional)
300 g (10½ oz/2 cups) unsalted
    shelled pistachios
100 g (3½ oz/1 cup) walnuts
100 g (3½ oz) brown sugar
1 teaspoon ground cardamom
large pinch of sea salt
125 g (4½ oz/½ cup) dairy-free butter or
    coconut oil, or use 125 ml (4 fl oz/½ cup)
    light-tasting olive oil
375 g (13 oz) refrigerated dairy-free filo
    pastry (about 20–24 sheets)

Instead of brushing butter straight onto the filo, channel your best Jackson Pollock impression and splatter it on. Tap excess butter from the brush and then spread to avoid oversaturated pieces of pastry. Pistachios command centre stage in this baklava so don't be stingy.

Mix the honey, sugar, zest (if using) and 170 ml (5½ fl oz/⅔ cup) water in a saucepan over medium heat. Gently heat the mixture and stir until the sugar has dissolved, then leave to simmer for 5 minutes. Remove from the heat and set aside to cool.

In a food processor, pulse the pistachios, walnuts, brown sugar, cardamom and salt into a rough rubble.

Melt the butter or coconut oil in a small saucepan over low heat (skip this step if using olive oil). Line a baking tin or dish with baking paper and rub the surface with a little of the butter or oil.

Preheat the oven to 200°C (400°F).

Remove the filo from the fridge and unfold it near the prepared tray. Move quickly, or wet and wring a tea towel almost dry and cover the filo to avoid it drying out. If needed, use kitchen scissors to trim the filo to the size of your baking tin.

Place a sheet of filo in the baking tin and use a pastry brush to splatter a little of the butter or oil over the top. Tap any excess butter or oil off the pastry, then use the pastry brush to spread it out in an even layer. Repeat with eight more sheets of filo to create your base layer.

Spread half the nut mixture over the filo. As the number of sheets in a packet of filo can vary, count how many you have left. You will need nine sheets for the top layer, so use however many are remaining for your middle layer, repeating the buttering process. Top with the remaining nut mixture.

Brush the remaining nine sheets of filo with butter or oil and place on top of the final layer of nuts. Using a paring knife and pressing down on the filo around the knife, diagonally score the baklava into diamonds. Brush any remaining butter or oil over the top.

Transfer the tin to the oven and immediately reduce the temperature to 170°C (340°F). Bake for 40 minutes or until golden.

Remove the baklava from the oven and evenly pour over the prepared, cooled syrup. Return the baklava to the oven for 5 minutes, then remove and allow to cool to room temperature. Use a knife to separate the pieces and serve.

When dissolving the sugar, use a wooden spoon and don't stir the mixture again once the sugar has dissolved. When stirring the chocolate, don't use a wooden spoon – instead use silicone or metal utensils to avoid introducing moisture.

Pouring hot honeycomb onto a freezer-cold baking paper–lined tray stops the sugar temperature from increasing while helping the honeycomb form and set quickly.

Chocolate-covered honeycomb bars

Makes 6

Ingredients

3½ teaspoons bicarbonate of soda
(baking soda)
180 g (6½ oz/½ cup) Vegan honey
(see page 170) or golden syrup
220 g (8 oz/1 cup) granulated sugar
200 g (7 oz) vegan dark chocolate, broken
into large pieces

You may know honeycomb as cinder toffee, hokey pokey, or as that one really fun experiment from primary school science class. Whatever form it comes in, it's astoundingly easy to make with the help of a candy thermometer. When set, you can smash it with a hammer or finesse it into chocolate bars. The forgiving embrace of melted chocolate means either way, they'll end up beautiful and delicious by the time you're done.

Line a baking tray with baking paper and set aside in the freezer to chill.

Sift the bicarb soda into a bowl and place it near the stove.

Pour the honey into a saucepan set over medium–low heat. Add the sugar and stir with a wooden spoon until the sugar has dissolved. Do not stir the mixture again.

Using a candy thermometer to assist you, slowly bring the mixture to 150°C (300°F). Do not let the mixture go above this temperature, otherwise it will burn. Remove the saucepan from the heat.

Immediately tip in the sifted bicarb soda and stir vigorously with a wooden spoon. Quickly pour the hot mixture onto the prepared tray, then immediately fill the pan with water to avoid any leftover mixture setting. Allow the honeycomb to cool at room temperature for at least 1 hour.

Once the honeycomb is cool, use a serrated knife to cut it into six chocolate-bar shapes. If you prefer, or you screw this step up along the way, you can smash the honeycomb into large chunks.

Place a heatproof bowl over a saucepan of simmering water. Add the chocolate to the bowl and stir until melted. Carefully remove the bowl from the heat and wipe off any condensation on the outside of the bowl.

Dip the honeycomb into the chocolate one at a time, until completely covered. Use a fork to lift the bars out of the chocolate, allowing any excess to drip off. Place the chocolate bars back on the baking paper and set aside to completely set. The bars will keep in an airtight container in the fridge for as long as you can keep your hands off them (which won't be long!).

Chai ice cream

Ingredients

280 ml (9½ fl oz) soy milk
140 g (5 oz/¾ cup) brown sugar
¼ teaspoon ground cloves
1 teaspoon ground cardamom
1 teaspoon ground ginger
2 teaspoons ground cinnamon
1½ tablespoons natural vanilla extract
½ teaspoon sea salt
pinch of guar gum or xanthan gum
2 chai or black tea bags

Ice cream

185 ml (6½ fl oz/¾ cup) soy milk
1 tablespoon freshly squeezed lemon juice
50 g (1¾ oz/½ cup) soy milk powder
55 g (2 oz/¼ cup) coconut oil
2 tablespoons sunflower oil

A proper chai latte is deliciously spiced, unlike its distant cousin the turmeric latte, which is simply a bland curry that someone forgot to add the rest of the ingredients to. That's why the former makes delicious ice cream and the latter is unwelcome in this book.

Place the milk, sugar, cloves, cardamom, ginger, cinnamon, vanilla, salt and gum in a saucepan and bring to the boil over medium heat. Turn the heat off, add the tea bags and steep with the lid on for 15 minutes. Remove the lid and allow to cool before removing the tea bags.

To make the ice cream, place the milk, lemon juice and milk powder in a blender and briefly blend together. With the motor running, slowly add the coconut and sunflower oils until the mixture becomes thick. Add the cooled chai mixture and blend again until combined. Transfer the mixture to the fridge until completely chilled.

Place the mixture in an ice-cream machine and churn according to the manufacturer's instructions for 25–30 minutes. Pour the ice cream into a freezer-friendly container and cover the surface of the ice cream with plastic wrap. Make sure the container is airtight to avoid ice crystals forming.

Freeze overnight, then scoop and serve.

Baklava fro-yo

Ingredients

1 kg (2 lb 3 oz) coconut yoghurt

260 g (9 oz/¾ cup) Vegan honey
(see page 170)

generous pinch of guar gum or
xanthan gum

500 g (1 lb 2 oz) Baklava (see page 144),
roughly chopped

You've come this far. You made the honey from scratch. You've turned that honey into syrup and drowned freshly baked baklava in it. You're mere steps away from recreating my baklava fro-yo, the most popular flavour from my ice-cream pop-up days – now yours to win hearts with.

Combine the coconut yoghurt, three-quarters of the honey and the gum in a large bowl and mix until smooth. Transfer the mixture to an ice-cream machine and churn according to the manufacturer's instructions for 25–30 minutes.

Pour the ice cream into a freezer-friendly airtight container and quickly stir in the baklava chunks. Swirl in the remaining honey, then smooth the surface of the ice cream with the back of a spoon and press plastic wrap over the surface to prevent ice crystals from forming. Place in the freezer for 12 hours to completely set.

Scoop and serve with a piece of left-over baklava if there's any left by then.

Overloaded chocolate bark

Ingredients

2 tablespoons olive oil

60 g (2 oz/¼ cup) popcorn kernels

sea salt

185 ml (6½ fl oz¾ cup) maple syrup

60 g (2 oz/¼ cup) cashew butter

1 teaspoon natural vanilla extract

400 g (14 oz) vegan dark or milk chocolate, broken into chunks

30 g (1 oz) pretzels or salted potato chips (crisps)

Finally a dessert for people who want shortcuts. In this recipe, cheat's caramel popcorn and a big handful of pretzels get coated in melted dark chocolate and left to set as big chunks of bark. Swap in vegan-friendly candies or marshmallows, salted potato chips or chunks of honeycomb. It's all good.

Preheat the oven to 160°C (320°F). Line a baking tray with baking paper.

Heat the olive oil in a small saucepan over medium–high heat for 3 minutes. Add a few popcorn kernels; if they start bubbling then the oil is almost ready and if they start popping then it's time to go. Add the rest of the kernels, then cover and cook the popcorn, shaking the pan from time to time, until the popping sound subsides. Remove from the heat, toss in ¼ teaspoon salt, then tip onto the prepared tray and spread out in a single layer. Set aside to cool.

Place the maple syrup in a small saucepan over medium heat. Using a candy thermometer to assist you, heat the maple syrup to 110°C (230°F). Immediately remove from the heat and allow to cool for 15 minutes. Stir in the cashew butter, ¾ teaspoon salt and the vanilla until smooth.

Pour the maple syrup mixture over the popcorn and stir until evenly distributed. Put the popcorn in the oven and bake for 8 minutes, stirring halfway through. Remove and set aside to cool.

Place a heatproof bowl over a saucepan of simmering water. Add the chocolate to the bowl and stir until melted and smooth. Carefully remove the bowl from the heat and wipe off any condensation on the outside of the bowl.

If you have any available work surface left by this stage, lay out a large sheet of baking paper. Pour most of the melted chocolate onto the paper into a 25 cm x 15 cm (10 in x 6 in) rectangle before covering in the caramel popcorn and as many of the pretzels or potato chips that will fit. Pour the remaining chocolate over the top, drizzling it into as many crevices as possible. Set aside in the fridge to set until hard.

Crack into chunk-sized bark pieces and keep in the fridge.

For a gluten-free version of this dessert, use soda water (club soda) instead of beer and replace the flour with gluten-free flour.

Beer-battered chocolate bars

Ingredients

4 vegan chocolate bars (about 50 g/1¾ oz each)
canola oil, for deep-frying
75 g (2¾ oz/½ cup) self-raising flour (see Note)
sea salt and freshly ground black pepper
125 ml (4 fl oz/½ cup) chilled beer (see Note)

Suggested toppings

sea salt flakes
vegan chocolate sauce
vegan chocolate cookies, broken into chunks
soy or rice whip
pretzels

There's something about a beer-battered, deep-fried block of chocolate for dessert that can't be topped. But go for it and top it with ice cream as well. This is one of the few recipes that I occasionally look at and think, well, that's a bit much. Eat while sitting down with your next of kin notified as the calorie coma can set in almost immediately.

Place the chocolate bars in the freezer for 2–3 hours to firm up.

Heat the canola oil in a large heavy-based saucepan over medium–high heat. Test if the oil is ready by inserting a wooden skewer or the handle of a wooden spoon into the oil; if it begins to bubble quickly then you're ready to go.

Place the flour in a small bowl and season with salt and pepper. Toss the frozen chocolate bars in the flour to lightly coat, then remove and set aside on a plate.

Pour the beer into the flour, stirring constantly, to create a batter. You may not need it all, so go slowly until the batter is runny but not so runny that it won't cling to the chocolate. Dip each chocolate bar into the batter until completely coated. One at a time, scoop the bars out with as much batter as you can keep clinging to them, then bravely drop the battered bars into the oil. Cook for 2–3 minutes, until golden brown and crisp.

Remove the chocolate bars using a slotted spoon and drain on paper towel. Serve warm with a sprinkling of fat sea salt flakes, chocolate sauce, chocolate cookies, soy or rice whip and a few pretzels, or whatever sweet garnishes you have lying around.

Dulce de leche tarts

Ingredients

150 g (5½ oz) tinned dairy-free condensed milk or dulce de leche

200–250 g (7–9 oz) vegan dark chocolate, broken into chunks

large sea salt flakes, for sprinkling (optional)

South American caramel, dulce de leche, can be made from a tin of condensed milk or purchased in most places condensed milk is available. Chocolate and fat sea salt flakes are all that are needed to turn it into a tart, which most agree is more socially acceptable than scooping the dulce de leche right out of the tin. Don't let that stop you though.

If using a tin of condensed milk, bring a very large saucepan of water to the lowest boil possible. Peel the label off the tin before placing it at the bottom of the pan on its side so it can roll around and not trap any air bubbles. Gently simmer for 3–4 hours (the longer you cook it the thicker your dulce de leche will be), making sure the water level doesn't go below the tin. Roll the tin around occasionally to remove any air bubbles. Remove the pan from the heat and allow to cool to room temperature before removing and opening the tin. Ta-da! That's dulce de leche.

Place a heatproof bowl over a saucepan of simmering water. Add the chocolate to the bowl and stir until melted and smooth. Carefully remove the bowl from the heat and wipe off any condensation on the outside of the bowl.

Place six paper cases into the holes of a muffin tin and spoon half the melted chocolate among the cases. Tilt the tin so the chocolate fully covers the base of each paper case. Place the muffin tin in the freezer for 5 minutes.

Spread the dulce de leche over the chocolate bases, before topping with the remaining chocolate. Return to the freezer for at least 15 minutes to fully set.

Sprinkle the tarts with sea salt flakes if you like, and keep in the fridge until serving.

Pumpkin pie

Ingredients

300 ml (10½ fl oz) dairy-free
  whipping cream
cinnamon sugar, for sprinkling

Filling

425 g (15 oz) pumpkin purée or 700 g
  (1 lb 9 oz) fresh pumpkin, quartered
125 g (4½ oz/⅔ cup) brown sugar
125 ml (4 fl oz/½ cup) soy milk
2½ tablespoons arrowroot
1½ teaspoons coconut oil
1 teaspoon natural vanilla extract
1 teaspoon ground cinnamon
¾ teaspoon ground ginger
½ teaspoon freshly grated nutmeg
¼ teaspoon ground cloves
¼ teaspoon sea salt

Shortcrust pastry

150 g (5½ oz) dairy-free butter, partially
  frozen, plus extra for greasing
350 g (12½ oz) plain (all-purpose) flour
1¼ teaspoons sea salt
¼ teaspoon granulated sugar
4–6 tablespoons ice-cold water (I usually
  use just over 5)

Pumpkin infiltrates enemy lines in this pie,
sneaking into the sweets chapter by wearing
a pumpkin spice mask that looks suspiciously
like chai spice. This double-agent dessert gets
away with it using a superb shortcrust disguise
and enough cream on top to bribe anyone with
remaining doubts.

If using fresh pumpkin, preheat the oven to 200°C (400°F). Line a baking tray with baking paper.

Place the pumpkin on the tray and bake for 45 minutes, flipping halfway through cooking. Remove the pumpkin when a fork easily pierces the flesh. Set aside to cool slightly, then peel the skin and discard. Transfer the pumpkin to a food processor and process for 3–4 minutes, until completely smooth. Increase the oven temperature to 220°C (430°F).

To make the shortcrust pastry, mash the butter with a few tablespoons of the flour in a large bowl until you make a paste. Mix in the rest of the flour along with the salt and sugar and use two forks to cut the butter paste into the flour. Continue until the butter is fully incorporated and the mixture resembles breadcrumbs.

Add the ice-cold water 1 tablespoon at a time, mixing thoroughly before adding any more. You want to use as little water as possible, so add it sparingly. When the dough just comes together, knead it once or twice to create a dough ball. The cold water and minimal kneading will stop any gluten forming, helping to make a crisp crust.

Grease an 18 cm (7 in) pie tin with butter.

Using your hands or a rolling pin, press or roll out the dough into a circle that's larger than your pie tin. Carefully lift the pastry into the tin and press it into place.

To make the filling, place the ingredients in a blender and blend until smooth. Spoon the mixture into the pastry case and tap the tin on your work surface to release any air bubbles.

Curve or fold any excess pastry (or trim it, as you may not need it all) over the pumpkin filling to create a thick rim. If you like, use a fork to create a pattern around the edge.

Bake the pie for 15 minutes, then reduce the temperature to 175°C (345°F) and bake for a further 35 minutes, rotating the tin halfway through cooking.

Remove the pie from the oven and allow to cool completely in the tin.

Using electric beaters, whip the cream until it's firm enough to create a cute twist, then spoon it onto the pumpkin pie in a decorative fashion. Sprinkle cinnamon sugar over the top and serve.

BASICS

Falafel

Ingredients

300 g (10½ oz) dried chickpeas (garbanzo
    beans), rinsed and soaked in cold water
    overnight
1 onion, roughly chopped
6 garlic cloves, peeled
splash of olive oil
1 teaspoon ground cumin
1 bunch flat-leaf parsley, leaves picked
1 bunch coriander (cilantro), leaves picked
55 g (2 oz/½ cup) chickpea flour (besan)
1⅓ teaspoons sea salt
½ teaspoon baking powder
⅓ teaspoon ground cardamom
⅓ teaspoon cayenne pepper
⅓ teaspoon ground coriander
generous squeeze of lemon juice
canola oil, for shallow-frying

Drain and rinse the chickpeas, then set aside on a clean tea towel to completely dry.

In a food processor, pulse the onion and garlic until they form a paste.

Heat the olive oil in a frying pan over medium–low heat. Add the onion and garlic paste and sauté for 10–15 minutes, until soft and translucent. Towards the end of the cooking time, add the cumin and stir through. Remove from the heat and set aside.

Finely process the chickpeas in the food processor, stopping just before they start to become a paste, but making sure there are no larger pieces of chickpea left. Add the parsley and coriander leaves and process until well combined.

Transfer the chickpea mixture to a large bowl and add the onion mixture, along with the remaining ingredients apart from the oil. Set aside in the fridge for at least 30 minutes to firm up.

When you're ready to fry, heat 5 cm (2 in) of canola oil in a frying pan over medium–high heat. Test if the oil is ready by inserting a wooden skewer or the handle of a wooden spoon into the oil; if it begins to bubble quickly then you're ready to go.

Use your hands to grab small amounts of the falafel mix and roll into tight, small balls. A good general rule is to make them no bigger than what you can hold in one very tight fistful or less.

Fry the falafel in batches of six, turning frequently, for 3–4 minutes, until golden brown. Using a slotted spoon, transfer to a plate lined with paper towel to drain.

Serve immediately.

Seitan chickpea chicken

Ingredients

270 g (9½ oz) gluten flour
2 tablespoons onion powder
4 teaspoons torula yeast (optional)
20 g (¾ oz) nutritional yeast
1 tablespoon ground sage
2 teaspoons dried thyme
1 teaspoon dried rosemary
½ teaspoon white pepper
55 g (2 oz/½ cup) chickpea flour (besan)
2 teaspoons olive oil
3 tablespoons white miso
2 tablespoons vegan Worcestershire sauce
2 tablespoons chicken-style stock powder

Combine the gluten flour, onion powder, torula yeast (if using), nutritional yeast, sage, thyme, rosemary and white pepper in a bowl. Make a well in the middle.

Place the chickpea flour, olive oil and 155 ml (5 fl oz) water in a blender and blend until smooth.

Place the miso, Worcestershire sauce, stock powder and 250 ml (8½ fl oz/1 cup) water in a saucepan and bring to the boil. Once boiling, pour in the blended chickpea mixture, remove from the heat and stir vigorously with a wooden spoon until glossy.

Pour the chickpea mixture into the bowl with the gluten flour mixture and stir with the spoon to incorporate. Stretch out the mixture and punch it down, repeating to knead for 3 minutes. The dough should be slightly sticky, stretchy and with visible strands of gluten formed. Pinch off 2.5 cm (1 in) chunks (or your desired size remembering the seitan will double in size during cooking) and loosely wrap the chunks in food-grade plastic wrap.

Place the seitan in a steamer set over a saucepan of simmering water and steam for 40 minutes, until doubled in size. Remove from the steamer and set aside to cool.

Once cooled, tear the seitan into strips to make shredded chicken or cut into chunks. To use in recipes, marinate and cook as you would regular chicken.

Rice paper bacon

Ingredients

2 tablespoons mushroom soy sauce
   or dark soy sauce
2 tablespoons olive oil
3 tablespoons nutritional yeast
1 teaspoon liquid smoke
1 tablespoon vegan Worcestershire sauce
1 tablespoon brown sugar
½ teaspoon smoked or hot paprika
½ teaspoon onion powder
½ teaspoon garlic powder
18 rice paper sheets
canola oil, for deep-frying or cooking
   oil spray

Combine all the ingredients except the rice paper and oil in a wide shallow bowl large enough to fit the rice paper.

Working with one rice paper sheet at a time, briefly rinse the sheets under cold running water until they are flexible enough to bend. You'll notice they become flexible very quickly, so you need to work fast. If you want to make more chewy 'bacon', press two rice paper sheets together to make nine sheets. Transfer the sheets to a work surface and use a clean tea towel to blot off excess water.

Dip the wet rice paper sheets into the marinade and wipe off any excess so that each side is evenly coated before placing on a plate. Alternatively, use your hands to rub the marinade into each side. If you want it to look like bacon, use scissors to cut it into strips.

If you're making crispy rice paper bacon, heat enough oil for deep-frying in a large heavy-based saucepan over medium heat. Test if the oil is ready by inserting a wooden skewer or the handle of a wooden spoon into the oil; if it begins to bubble quickly then you're ready to go. Add the rice paper sheets and fry for 20 seconds, using tongs to keep the sheets from curling into a ball and flipping halfway through. Drain on a plate lined with paper towel.

If you're making chewy rice paper bacon, lightly spray a frying pan with cooking oil spray and set over medium heat. Add the rice paper sheets and cook, flipping halfway through, for 1–2 minutes or until both sides are bubbling and starting to char. Using tongs, give the bacon a little pinch to create a more bacon-like shape. Drain on a plate lined with paper towel.

For both methods, do not take your eyes off your bacon as it cooks – there is a fine line between slightly charry goodness and burnt crisps!

Serve your rice paper bacon on the side of a big breakfast, cut up into strips and add to dishes for a smoky flavour or store in an airtight container for an on-the-go salty snack!

Mayonnaise

Ingredients

60 ml (2 fl oz/¼ cup) soy milk or
   3 tablespoons aquafaba + 1 tablespoon
   tinned chickpeas (garbanzo beans)
¾ teaspoon apple cider vinegar or
   white vinegar
¼ teaspoon American or Dijon mustard
¼ teaspoon garlic powder
¼ teaspoon sea salt
185 ml (6½ fl oz/¾ cup) canola oil or other
   neutral-flavoured oil

Place all the ingredients except the oil in the bowl of a stick blender or plastic jug. Blend with a stick blender for 20 seconds or so, until frothy.

With the stick blender running, slowly pour in the oil in a steady stream for 1–2 minutes, until you have an emulsified and thick mayonnaise. Taste, and adjust the seasoning if necessary.

The mayonnaise will keep in an airtight container in the fridge for up to 4 weeks.

Japanese mayonnaise

Ingredients

60 ml (2 fl oz/¼ cup) soy milk
1 teaspoon American or Dijon mustard
½ teaspoon MSG
½ teaspoon kala namak (Indian black salt),
   plus extra if needed
¼ teaspoon finely chopped nori
2 teaspoons apple cider vinegar, plus
   extra if needed
1 teaspoon granulated sugar, plus extra
   if needed
185 ml (6½ fl oz/¾ cup) canola oil or other
   neutral-flavoured oil

Place all the ingredients except the oil in the bowl of a stick blender or plastic jug. Blend with a stick blender for 20 seconds or so until frothy.

With the stick blender running, slowly pour in the oil in a steady stream for 1–2 minutes, until you have you have an emulsified and thick mayonnaise. Adjust to taste with more kala namak, vinegar or sugar if necessary.

The mayonnaise will keep in an airtight container in the fridge for up to 5 days.

Tzatziki mayonnaise

Ingredients

½ long cucumber, halved lengthways

1 x quantity Mayonnaise (see page 165 or use store-bought vegan mayonnaise)

1 tablespoon freshly squeezed lemon juice

½ teaspoon minced garlic

¼ teaspoon garlic powder

½ bunch dill, fronds picked and finely chopped

Using a teaspoon, scrape out the cucumber seeds and discard. Grate the remaining cucumber and squeeze the liquid into a bowl. Set aside the cucumber flesh.

Add the mayonnaise, lemon juice, minced garlic and garlic powder to the cucumber liquid and stir well to combine. Add the dill and reserved cucumber flesh and mix until combined.

Set aside in the fridge, ideally overnight, before using to allow the flavours to intensify, but if you haven't planned ahead it won't hurt to skip this part and just go for it.

Store any leftovers in an airtight container in the fridge for 2–3 days.

Ranch dipping sauce

Ingredients

60 ml (2 fl oz/¼ cup) soy milk
2 teaspoons freshly squeezed lemon juice
1 x quantity Mayonnaise (see page 165 or
   use store-bought vegan mayonnaise)
2 tablespoons snipped chives
1 teaspoon finely chopped flat-leaf parsley
   leaves or dill fronds
½ teaspoon garlic powder
½ teaspoon Dijon or American mustard
¼ teaspoon onion powder
¼ teaspoon sea salt
small pinch of paprika
freshly ground black pepper, to taste

Make a basic buttermilk by combining the soy milk and lemon juice in a large bowl. Set aside for a few minutes to thicken. Stir through the remaining ingredients, then taste and adjust the flavours if necessary to suit your taste.

Tartar sauce

Ingredients

230 g (8 oz) dill pickles (gherkins), finely chopped

2 tablespoons finely chopped dill fronds

265 g (9½ oz/1 cup) Mayonnaise (see page 165 or use store-bought vegan mayonnaise)

2 teaspoons freshly squeezed lemon juice, or to taste

1 teaspoon Dijon or American mustard, or to taste

1 teaspoon caper brine, or to taste

Combine the dill pickle and dill in a small bowl. Stir through the mayonnaise until well combined. Gradually add the remaining ingredients, tasting and adjusting the flavour as you go until you reach a balance you are happy with.

Cover and store in the fridge for at least 1 week. Serve with the Crabless cakes on page 37, the Mushroom po'boys on page 64 or alongside the 'Fish' and chips on page 97.

To make this cream cheese even more spectacular, make a dill cream cheese by adding the zest and juice of 1 lemon, 2 teaspoons of capers along with 2 teaspoons of brine from the jar and a garlic clove to the cream cheese mixture before processing to combine. Add a large handful of dill fronds and process briefly, then store in an airtight container in the fridge for up to 1 week.

Sour cream

Ingredients

200 g (7 oz) raw cashews or 160 g (5½ oz) sunflower seeds, soaked overnight in cold water and drained
½ teaspoon citric acid
1 teaspoon onion powder
½ teaspoon sea salt
2 tablespoons freshly squeezed lemon juice
1 teaspoon arrowroot powder
1 tablespoon olive oil
⅓ teaspoon garlic powder

Place the nuts or seeds in a food processor and process until smooth, scraping down the side of the bowl as needed. Add the remaining ingredients and continue to process until very smooth.

Transfer the mixture to a bowl and set aside in the fridge for 2 hours before serving. If the sour cream separates, give it a gentle stir to bring it back to working order.

The sour cream will keep in an airtight container in the fridge for up to 1 week.

Cream cheese

Ingredients

400 g (14 oz) raw cashews
150 g (5½ oz) dairy-free yoghurt
2 teaspoons lactic acid (or ½ teaspoon citric acid)
1 teaspoon sea salt, plus extra if needed
2 teaspoons white vinegar, plus extra if needed
1 tablespoon nutritional yeast, plus extra if needed

Soak the cashews in plenty of cold water for at least 8 hours, or boil for 15 minutes, then drain and set aside to cool.

Place the cashews in a food processor and process for 1 minute, scraping down the side of the bowl as necessary. Add the yoghurt and continue to process until the mixture becomes smooth.

Add the remaining ingredients, then taste and adjust the flavour if necessary, adding more salt, vinegar or nutritional yeast. Process for a few more seconds – you'll know it's ready when the cheese is creamy without any graininess from the nuts.

Transfer to an airtight container and store in the fridge for up to 1 week.

Vegan honey

Ingredients

2 litres (68 fl oz/8 cups) fresh, cloudy or long-life apple juice

880 g (1 lb 15 oz/4 cups) granulated sugar

4 teaspoons carob syrup (see Note)

You can buy carob syrup from most health-food stores and online.

Place the apple juice in a saucepan and bring to the boil over medium heat. Simmer, maintaining a low boil, for about 45 minutes or until the apple juice has reduced by half. If using fresh or cloudy apple juice, frequently skim the surface to remove any sediment that rises to the top. Use this time to bask in how fantastic your kitchen smells right now.

In a separate saucepan, bring 1 litre (34 fl oz/4 cups) water to the boil over medium heat. Stir in the sugar and stir for 3 minutes or until the sugar has dissolved. Pour the sugar syrup into the reduced apple juice.

Keep the sweetened apple juice bubbling for 1–1½ hours, until the liquid has reduced to about 750 ml (25½ fl oz/3 cups) and resembles a honey-like thickness. Use a candy thermometer to keep an eye on the temperature; if it goes over 112°C (234°F) the final product will be firmer than a syrup and it won't work as a pourable honey.

Remove the pan from the heat and stir in the carob syrup. Allow to cool before pouring into sterilised jars for storage. The honey will keep in the pantry for several months.

Chocolate hazelnut spread

Makes 660 g (1 lb 7 oz/2½ cups)

Ingredients

420 g (15 oz/3 cups) hazelnuts
85 g (3 oz/⅔ cup) cocoa powder
25 g (1 oz/¼ cup) soy milk powder
 (optional)
¼ teaspoon sea salt
185 g (6½ oz/1½ cups) pure icing
 (confectioners') sugar
up to 1½ tablespoons refined coconut oil

Preheat the oven to 180°C (350°F).

Place the hazelnuts on a baking tray lined with baking paper and roast for 10–12 minutes, until aromatic.

Place the hazelnuts in a clean tea towel, wrap up and allow them to steam for a few minutes. Rub the nuts in the tea towel until the skins loosen or transfer to a metal colander and use the towel to vigorously rub the skins off. Scavenge out the skinned hazelnuts and discard the skins.

While the hazelnuts are still warm, transfer to a food processor and process for 15 minutes, scraping the side of the bowl occasionally, or until the hazelnuts have transformed into a butter.

Add the cocoa powder, soy milk powder (if using) and salt and briefly process. With the processor running, slowly add the icing sugar. The mixture may eventually clump together into a ball, but this is OK.

With the processor still running, add the coconut oil in small increments until you're satisfied with the consistency – the final spread will be slightly less runny once it has fully cooled.

Store the hazelnut spread in a jar in the pantry for up to 2 months.

When you make the hazelnut butter, make sure the hazelnuts are warm so they release their oils more quickly. Process until completely smooth if you want to replicate the consistency of the classic – it's ready when it's noticeably oily and the mixture is almost pulverised to a liquid.

Index

Index

Smith Street Books

Published in 2020 by Smith Street Books
Naarm | Melbourne | Australia
smithstreetbooks.com

ISBN: 978-1-925811-39-1

Publisher: Paul McNally
Project manager: Aisling Coughlan
Editor: Lucy Heaver, Tusk Studio
Designer: Vaughan Mossop, Neighbourhood Creative
Photographer: Pete Dillon
Food stylist: Bridget Wald
Home economists: Zacchary Bird and Aisling Coughlan
Proofreader: Pam Dunne
Indexer: Helena Holmgren

Printed & bound in China by C&C Offset Printing Co., Ltd.

Book 129
10 9 8 7 6 5 4 3

Acknowledgements

I'd like to thank the people who have been instrumental in allowing me to put this book together. My family: Kerry, Nigel, Josh, Brittany, Tim, Charlotte, Ava, Betty, Rowan and Helen; and my friends: Megan J, Kevan P, Sven H, Rebecca B, Lea M (Paul and Mac, too!), Sara K, Bee S, Chris M, Sophie J, Dinesh M and so many others. Mostly, though, I'd like to thank the vegan community for welcoming everyone into a movement in favour of kindness, where we work towards a world full of compassionate junk food. So sit back with a glass of wine and a B12 supplement and have a flick through this book. I know you'll love the delicious food from around the world you're going to create with it. Kali orexi! Itadakimasu! Bone apple tea! Bon appetit! However you say it, please enjoy these recipes for everyone.

Cheers,
Zacchary Bird